Robotics for Pandemics

Robotics for Pandemics

Edited by

Hooman Samani

CRC Press
Taylor & Francis Group
Boca Raton London New York

CRC Press is an imprint of the
Taylor & Francis Group, an **informa** business

A CHAPMAN & HALL BOOK

First Edition published 2022
by CRC Press
6000 Broken Sound Parkway NW, Suite 300, Boca Raton, FL 33487-2742

and by CRC Press
2 Park Square, Milton Park, Abingdon, Oxon, OX14 4RN

CRC Press is an imprint of Taylor & Francis Group, LLC

Library of Congress Cataloging-in-Publication Data

Names: Samani, Hooman, editor.
Title: Robotics for pandemics / edited by Hooman Samani.
Description: First edition. | Boca Raton : CRC Press, 2022. | Includes
bibliographical references and index.
Identifiers: LCCN 2021036782 | ISBN 9781032048734 (hardback) |
ISBN 9781032048963 (paperback) | ISBN 9781003195061 (ebook)
Subjects: LCSH: Robotics in medicine. | Epidemics.
Classification: LCC R859.7.C67 R63 2022 | DDC 610.285--dc23
LC record available at https://lccn.loc.gov/2021036782

ISBN: 978-1-032-04873-4 (hbk)
ISBN: 978-1-032-04896-3 (pbk)
ISBN: 978-1-003-19506-1 (ebk)

DOI: 10.1201/9781003195061

Typeset in Minion Pro
by KnowledgeWorks Global Ltd.

Contents

About the Editor

Hooman Samani is a Lecturer in Machine Learning, AI for Robotics at the School of Engineering, Computing and Mathematics, University of Plymouth, United Kingdom. He has worked as an associate professor and is the founder and director of the AIART (Artificial Intelligence and Robotics Technology Laboratory) lab at National Taipei University of Taiwan. He holds a PhD degree in Robotics from the National University of Singapore (NUS) and has worked as a Research Fellow at the Keio-NUS CUTE Centre, a joint research centre between NUS and Keio University of Japan. He is actively serving on several robotics and AI related journals and conferences as an editorial board member, organising committee member, workshop organizer and reviewer. Apart from academia, he has work experience in Philips and Posco as well as R&D projects in different industrial sectors that have rounded-out his experiences. He was featured in many international media such as Discovery Channel, New Scientist and Reuters, starring his research in the emerging field of Cognitive Robotics. In tandem with his research in robotics, he has participated and won several international RoboCup competitions.

Contributors

Abid Haleem

Department of Mechanical Engineering, Jamia Millia Islamia, New Delhi, India

Prof. Abid Haleem is a Professor of Mechanical Engineering in Jamia Millia Islamia, New Delhi, India. He has published more than 200 SCOPUS/SCI indexed research papers in refereed international and national journals such as Resources Policy, Benchmarking: An International Journal, Production Planning and Control, International Journal of Logistic Systems and Management, Journal of Enterprise Information Management, Journal of Cleaner Production, International Journal of Business Excellence, Global Journal of Flexible Systems Management, Renewable and Sustainable Energy, Energy Review, etc. Has more than 32 years of teaching, consulting, research and development experience in varied areas such as additive manufacturing, supply chain management, innovation, sustainability, technology management and allied areas of industrial engineering. He holds good administrative experience with industry and academia.

Mohd Javaid

Department of Mechanical Engineering, Jamia Millia Islamia, New Delhi, India

Dr. Mohd Javaid is an Assistant Professor of Mechanical Engineering, Faculty of Engineering, Jamia Millia Islamia, New Delhi. He graduated in Mechanical Engineering from Government College of Engineering and Technology, Jammu and received his Master's in Industrial and Production Engineering from NIT Kurukshetra, India. He obtained his PhD in the area of Additive Manufacturing from Jamia Millia Islamia, New Delhi and has published more than 90 research papers in Scopus/

SCI Indexed journals and five in international conferences. His other research interests are in Industry 4.0.

Arnon Jumlongkul
School of Medicine, Mae Fah Luang University, Chiang Rai, Thailand
Arnon Jumlongkul is a lecturer and a forensic doctor at the School of Medicine, Mae Fah Luang University in Chiang Rai, Thailand. Sukhothai Thammathirat Open University awarded him a Bachelor and Master of Laws degree (Criminal Law and Criminal Justice), and Naresuan University awarded him a Doctor of Medicine degree. He received a Higher Graduate Diploma of Clinical Sciences Degree (Forensic Medicine) from Chulalongkorn University as well as a Diploma of the Thai Board of Forensic Medicine from the Medical Council of Thailand. His primary responsibilities include teaching legal medicine, medical laws and medical innovation to undergraduate students. He also conducts forensic investigations, sits on the Mae Fah Luang University Ethics Committee and creates biomedical inventions.

Sini Kolari
Faculty of Information Technology, University of Jyväskylä, Finland
Sini Kolari is a designer and an entrepreneur with a BA degree in Crafts and Design from the Lahti Institute of Design and Fine Arts. She is currently studying for a Master's degree in Information Systems at the University of Jyväskylä. She is aiming to bring her experience in emotional design and entrepreneurship into the realm of digital innovation and technology.

Roman Lakovlev
St. Petersburg Federal Research Center of the Russian Academy of Sciences (SPC RAS), Russia
Roman is a researcher in the field of robotics, cyberphysical systems and data science. Currently he is an employee of Laboratory of Big Data Technologies of Sociocyberphysical Systems in St. Petersburg Federal Research Center of the Russian Academy of Sciences. His scientific career started from education at ITMO University, where he specialised in optics and computer vision. Graduated in 2017, he proceeded his education having entered St. Petersburg State University for the Master's degree in information business analytics. After completing

his studies in 2019, Roman concentrated on the problems of industrial implementation of robotic means, and later expanded his area of interest towards cyber-physical systems. To date, Roman is the author of over 30 scientific articles, holds several patents and has experience of participating in more than 7 research projects of various sizes. Since 2020, he has been the leader of a working group focused on research and development in the field of cyber-physical systems and data science.

Maksim Letenkov
St. Petersburg Federal Research Center of the Russian Academy of Sciences (SPC RAS), Russia
Maksim is a graduate of SUAI. He received a Master's degree in Mechatronics and Robotics in 2019. Currently, Maksim is engaged in research on the problems of artificial intelligence in the laboratory of big data technologies of socio-cyber-physical systems SPC RAS.

Chunxu Li
Centre for Robotics and Neural Systems, University of Plymouth, UK
Dr. Chunxu Li received the BE degree in engineering from the Qingdao University of Science and Technology, Qingdao, China in 2014, and the MSc degree in engineering and PhD degree in electrical and electronic engineering from Swansea University, Swansea, UK in 2016 and 2019, respectively. He is currently working as a Lecturer with the University of Plymouth. His research interests include robotics, automation and computational intelligence.

Shanay Rab
Department of Mechanical Engineering, Jamia Millia Islamia, New Delhi, India
Shanay Rab is a Mechanical Engineer, obtained his M. Tech from IIT (ISM), Dhanbad with a specialisation in Machine Design. He is currently a PhD scholar, doing joint research with
CSIR-National Physical Laboratory and JMI in the area of Pressure Metrology. He has published several scientific research papers in international and national journals and conference proceedings. His research interests include FEA, Machine Design, Pressure/Force Metrology and AM. He is also actively involved in science communication in the country.

Rebekah Rousi

School of Marketing and Communication, University of Vaasa; Gofore Plc;
Faculty of Information Technology, University of Jyväskylä, Finland

Rebekah Rousi holds a PhD in Cognitive Science, from the University of
Jyväskylä, Finland. Rousi's research focuses on human experience in
relation to technology from a broad range of perspectives including:
trust, ethics, emotions, human–robot interaction, human-AI interaction,
embodied and multisensory user experience, learning technology and
more. Rousi approaches research through the mind of an artist. She
applies her earlier training and experience in visual art and cultural
studies to understand and represent human-technology interaction in a
narrative and performative way.

Anton Saveliev

St. Petersburg Federal Research Center of the Russian Academy of Sciences
(SPC RAS), Russia

Anton is a scientist in the field of robotics and the head of Laboratory
of Autonomous Robotic Systems in St. Petersburg Federal Research
Center of the Russian Academy of Sciences (SPC RAS). He is originally
from Kazan, Russia. He started his scientific career as a student of St.
Petersburg State University of Aerospace Instrumentation (SUAI),
specialising in Robots and Robotic Systems. Graduated in 2012, he
received an engineer's degree. In 2016, he defended his PhD thesis on
'Architectures, algorithms and software tools for processing multimodal
data streams in peer-to-peer web applications of video conferencing' in
SPC RAS, St. Petersburg, Russia. Anton is the author of over 80 scientific
papers and 6 patents. Since 2017, he is the head of the Laboratory of
Autonomous Robotic Systems, SPC RAS. In addition, since September
2017, he is a senior lecturer at the Department of Electromechanics and
Robotics in the SUAI.

Mohammad Shidujaman

Future Laboratory, Tsinghua University, China

Mohammad Shidujaman currently pursuing his PhD degree in Design
from the Academy of Arts and Design, Tsinghua University. He was a
visiting scholar at the Department of Electronic Engineering, Shibaura
Institute of Technology, Tokyo, Japan during his PhD study. His
current research interests include Human–Robot interaction, AI ethics,
Human-centric computing and Behavioral Analytics.

Sergey V. Shushardzhan

'The Scientific Research Center for Music Therapy and Healthcare Technologies' LLC, Moscow, Russia

Prof. Dr. Sergey V. Shushardzhan, MD, DMedSc, PhD, is an expert in rehabilitation, music therapy and medical robotics. By a second profession, he is a professional opera singer and vocal teacher. Dr. Shushardzhan is the author of 230 papers, textbooks, tutorials and monographs in music therapy, rehabilitation, medical robotics, cellular acoustics, anti-aging medicine, reflexology and psychology, founder of Scientific Music Therapy and Medical Bioacoustics with 11 patents for inventions.

Rajiv Suman

Department of Industrial & Production Engineering, G.B. Pant University of Agriculture & Technology, Pantnagar, Uttarakhand, India

Dr. Rajiv Suman is working as an Assistant Professor in the Department of Industrial and Production Engineering, College of Technology, G.B. Pant University of Agriculture & Technology, Pantnagar, Uttarakhand, India. He graduated in Bachelor of Technology (Production Engineering) from College of Technology, G.B. Pant University of Agriculture & Technology, Pantnagar, Uttarakhand in 2006. He did Master of Technology in Mechanical Engineering in 2012 with specialisation in Industrial & Production Engineering from National Institute of Technology, Kurukshetra (Haryana). He did his PhD degree in Mechanical Engineering from the department of Mechanical Engineering from College of Technology, G.B. Pant University of Agriculture and Technology, Pantnagar, Uttarakhand in 2015. He attended more than 20 short term courses, workshops, national & International seminars and conferences. With h index of 10 in google scholar and more than 800 citations has published more than 35 research articles of which many articles indexed in SCOPUS for National, International Journals and conferences. He has also organised various webinars and faculty development programmes.

Irina Vatamaniuk

St. Petersburg Federal Research Center of the Russian Academy of Sciences (SPC RAS), Russia

Irina is a graduate of SUAI. She received a Master's degree in 2014. Irina currently works as a researcher at the laboratory of Autonomous Robotic

Systems in St. Petersburg Federal Research Center of the Russian Academy of Sciences (SPC RAS). Her research interests are methods, algorithms and architecture of robotic and information control systems. Irina has also worked on image processing, computer vision and image quality assessment. Irina is the author of 64 scientific articles several registered computer programs.

Shuo Zhu

Centre for Robotics and Neural Systems, University of Plymouth, United Kingdom

Mr. Shuo Zhu obtained a Bachelor's degree in engineering from Heilongjiang University in 2017, and a Master's degree in mechanical engineering from Swansea University in 2020. Currently, he is studying for a PhD at Plymouth University, majoring in robotics and artificial intelligence.

CHAPTER 1

Robotics Applications for Public Health and Safety During the COVID-19 Pandemic

Mohd Javaid, Abid Haleem, and Shanay Rab

Department of Mechanical Engineering, Jamia
Millia Islamia, New Delhi, India

Rajiv Suman

Department of Industrial & Production Engineering, G.B. Pant
University of Agriculture & Technology, Pantnagar, India

CONTENTS

DOI: 10.1201/9781003195061-1

1

1.1 INTRODUCTION

Many countries all around the world remain locked due to the COVID-19 pandemic. People cannot leave their homes unless an emergency or need exists, such as shopping for food or buying vital products. Robotics is employed to supply patients with meals, communicate with patients and carry out everyday duties. This technology has a large number of functions and may provide valuable resources during an emergency in COVID-19. It can be used for disinfection, and to distribute critical products like food and medication, support border control and check the vital signs of humans. Mobile robotics influences lowering the risks of employees, medical expenditures and legal services costs. It enables workers to concentrate on complicated and gratifying activities [1–3].

Robotics is being used to communicate with patients from a safe distance in hospitals, with physicians and nurses, relatives and even receptionists. Specialised robots supply food and medicines to rooms, sanitise the rooms and handle concealed additional labour related to the patients. Infectious samples are carried to test laboratories by delivery robots. It uses disinfectant spray in public places outside hospitals, public works and public safety offices. Robots help in unforeseen ways both at work and at home. In hospitals with COVID-19 patients, health personnel may remotely apply their knowledge and compassion to unwell and isolated patients [4, 5].

Collaborative robots are one of the quickest automation options on the market, enabling new applications to be deployed. During the lockdown, many businesses must repurpose their assembly lines to concentrate on various goods based on their urgency of requirements. Here, robotics can be used to do the job of workers and avoid the spread of the infection. The extensive use of robots in COVID-19 shows that more robots are needed in the healthcare system and for doing daily tasks, as they do not need any personal protective equipment (PPE) and cannot get infected. COVID-19 hopefully speeds up the adoption and adaption of robots and may also lead to new robots [6, 7].

Manufacturing automation obstacles include plenty of unqualified work, a lack of shop floor spaciousness, or the absence of technical knowledge in the handling of sophisticated new technologies. Manufacturers may solve problems by employing robotics in their installations and assembly lines; by allowing people and machinery to operate concurrently, robotics decrease human touch, allowing them to maintain social distancing norms. Manufacturers use this technology in social distancing procedures at workplaces, generally worker-dense, thus allowing factories to remain busy while maintaining the safety of their personnel [8–10].

The shadow of the COVID-19 will probably remain for some time, and certain continuous adjustments will be required in the way enterprises operate. The current worldwide health crisis has caused several critical behavioural changes like social distancing, use of masks, avoidance of crowded areas, restrictions at everyday places, environment cleansing and disinfection and remote operations. The interest and demand for automation robots in several sectors are on the rise. Autonomous robots and their human capacity are also getting plenty of hype. In highly organised contexts, most robotics can do very simple jobs with a restricted range of automation. Recent advances in Artificial Intelligence (AI) and computer systems have accelerated the capacity of autonomous robots in unstructured environments to progressively carry out more complicated jobs [11, 12].

1.2 WHAT IS ROBOTICS?

Robotics is a field that combines science, engineering and technology to create devices called robots that do (or mimic) human behaviours. A robot is a product of the robotics industry, which involves creating programmable devices that can help people or replicate their behaviours. Robotics aims to create devices that can aid and support people. Mechanical engineering, electrical engineering, information engineering, mechatronics, electronics, bioengineering, computer engineering, control engineering, software engineering and mathematics are just a few areas that robotics encompasses. With numerous new general technical advances, the area of robotics has evolved significantly. One is the growth of big data, which provides additional opportunities for robotic systems to be programmed.

Another example is using new types of sensors and linked devices to monitor environmental factors such as temperature, air pressure, light, motion and other parameters. All of this contributes to the advancement of robotics and the development of more complicated and intelligent robots for various applications, including production, health and safety and human support. Artificial intelligence and robotics are both intertwined in the subject of robotics [13–15].

Robots are now seen to have their own intellect, although limited by their programming and capabilities because they are physically separate entities. Initially, robots were designed to perform repetitive jobs (such as producing automobiles on an assembly line), but they have since evolved to undertake jobs such as fighting fires, cleaning houses and aiding highly complex procedures. Each robot has a different amount of autonomy, ranging from fully autonomous bots that do activities without external influences to human-controlled bots that carry out activities that a person has complete control over [16, 17].

1.3 DIFFERENT TYPES OF ROBOTS HELPFUL DURING THE COVID-19 PANDEMIC

As the coronavirus emergency burst into a full-blown pandemic in the early 2020, causing many enterprises to close, robot-making enterprises found themselves in an unexpected situation. In the short term, robotics firms are rising to the occasion and delivering the solutions required to combat COVID-19 on the front lines. Cleaning and sanitising locations where humans are at risk are examples of applications. Mobile robots and drones are being refitted, repurposed and redeployed in certain situations, while robots developed for this function are being deployed in others [18, 19]. Robots do not require masks, can be readily cleaned and, of course, they do not get ill. When areas need to be watched to ensure that social distancing or lockdown standards are maintained, robots are also employed in a surveillance capacity.

In hospitals, robots also engage directly with symptomatic patients, collect their temperatures, do logistics duties and handle supplies. In a rush to identify a vaccine for COVID-19, robots are once again being used to handle samples and, in some instances, AI is being used to expedite data processing in the hopes of speeding up the development process. The present COVID-19 pandemic poses several risks and limitations for our civilisation [20–23]. Table 1.1 discusses some of the critical robotics applications during the COVID-19 pandemic.

1.4 KEY FEATURES OF ROBOTICS

Many key features and solutions are provided by robotics that can contribute to today's environment. Telepresence enables individuals to experience high quality video conferencing with people at any remote location. It allows families to keep in touch without jeopardising one another. It is essential in hospitals, particularly during the COVID-19 pandemic, as patients have lonely emotions. Robots do not have to be moved like a tablet, and they typically have built-in cameras and patients can use voice commands. The danger of viral infections is thereby reduced. Robots can assist hospitals in ensuring the observance of social distancing directives and provide solutions such as wearing masks, so that visitors, patients and

TABLE 1.1 Types of Robots Helpful during the COVID-19 Pandemic

S No	Types of Robots	How Are They Helpful in the COVID-19 Pandemic
1	Diagnosis robots	The robot's use begins with patient testing, as the robot can mass screen and quickly confirm COVID-19 instances. It can also perform swab tests with patients; a semi-automatic oropharyngeal swab robot has been designed. The swab robot is fitted with a remote camera, which allows the medical team to do the sampling with clear eyesight but without having to come into close touch with the patient.
2	Logistics robots	Robots play an important role in the transportation of materials and products, from service robots providing meals and other necessities to drones and mobility robots carrying medications and consumables like PPE. They have been used in warehouses and logistics facilities for some time, but they are now making their way into retail, where they can clean, disinfect, scan and refill shelves.
3	Manufacturing robots	Manufacturers sought to emphasise their teams' safety while keeping the wheels of industry spinning face problems due to social distancing standards. It is not simply a business issue: many firms manufacture critical PPE and medical equipment, such as ventilators.
4	Healthcare robots	Thus, to bridge the contacts between the patients and the care staff, a service robot has been designed. Medical robots can do simple tasks like delivering medicines and supplies, allowing carers to focus on more critical tasks. Serving robots, cleaning and spraying robots and surgical robots are all examples of robots that can be used in the healthcare system.
5	Disinfection robots	Disinfection robots should also perform cleaning tasks to avoid human-to-human interaction. In certain places, ultraviolet surface disinfection has been shown, with a 99.99% disinfection rate obtained in 15 minutes in a hospital wardroom. Because of its efficiency, safety and efficacy, disinfection robot orders are expected to increase by 400%–600%.
6	Social assistance robots	During the protracted fight against COVID-19, social isolation and loneliness are becoming more of a problem. New technologies, such as social robots, are being proposed to begin human-to-human relationships remotely to alleviate loneliness, decrease the danger of direct contact and share healthcare practitioners' burden. As a result, the receiver's general health can be improved.
7	Robots for tourism and hotel industry	Tourism and hospitality businesses utilise robots to help them overcome the adverse effects of social distancing limitations on their businesses. These robots are meant to give clients fewer frequent services.
8	Educational robots	Educational robots allow students of all ages to learn about robotics and programming while also developing other cognitive abilities.

staff wear their masks onsite. They can help turn attention to those who require particular care and help the employees utilise their time more efficiently [24, 25].

Drastic steps have become necessary with the new threat to mankind and civilisation due to COVID-19. The use of robots to combat this deadly infection is one such technique. One of the critical places for exposure is medical facilities with a high level of infection, where individuals who help other people and medical practitioners are at a high risk of acquiring infection. Due to the adaptability and support of robots, numerous care centres have begun testing and innovating robots and installing them in medical institutions. Robots and people might utilise synergies in the health sector and especially during a crisis. People and robots do a range of jobs connected to various intelligence kinds. Medical practitioners use robots to administer or measure medication for patients. It reduces interaction between humans and also reduces potential infections [26, 27].

1.5 AI-ENABLED ROBOTICS

AI approaches also help robotic devices that can be connected to the cloud in these devices. The knowledge of an AI-enabled robotic device may be uploaded via 'cloud robotics' to all other linked robots. The implications of AI-enabled applications in the workplace must be considered by occupational security and medical professionals, researchers, companies and employees. Comprehensive safety and health assessment of their advantages and hazards should be carried out before AI-enabled systems. Hospitals are moving to robots of different kinds to lower constant exposure between COVID-19 patients and disease carriers. It can be used to screen viral patients to reduce healthcare hazards remotely. AI-enabled robotics can deliver prospective advantages for occupational security practice and health as well as possible problems. Continued data from workplace sensors can be used to avoid hazardous exposures via early intervention. These data would enable practitioners to move from conventional dependence on slower episodes or sampling of breathing areas [28–30]. Robots with AI can assist in diagnosing and draw blood for sampling. They can also contribute to the supply of medications and critical products.

Additionally, healthcare, telecoms, online seminars, the processing of toxic waste and items, and other high-risk jobs for people may be helpful to robots. Many technical changes throughout history have entailed the substitution of human work for some kind of machinery. In certain areas, COVID-19 will undoubtedly speed up the process.

1.6 ROBOTICS FOR HEALTHCARE

Robotics reduces contact between healthcare workers and patients. In the context of a pandemic, robotics has long created solutions for the health system. This technology has been used to link physicians vocally and visually from afar with their patients in hospitals. Doctors are able to check their patients without spending time in travelling. Technology in the form of robots is now providing additional benefits by preventing direct physical contact with the sick. The way surgeons see COVID-19 essentially changes direct patient engagement. Sometimes robotics is presented by the related jobs as an adversary of humankind. In addition, employees, patients and stakeholders should be aware of the potential advantages of robotics.. Robotics delivery has proven highly helpful in times of health crisis and beyond and is one of the quickest delivery modules out today. It is used for cleaning and disinfection robots in many hospitals to cope with human resources shortages. Medical personnel are under much work pressure and, hopefully, robot assistants will provide help [31–33].

Robotics reduces infection chances through personal interaction, making it possible for physicians, nurses and other healthcare providers to focus their energy wherever best utilised. Robotics can clean hospital surfaces, provide patients with food and medications, support surgeons in precision operations under personal protection equipment restrictions, and more. Robots can relieve human work due to demand for hospital beds on a level that they have not seen before under normal circumstances. Transport of food supply to a patient's room: this use case was deemed especially intriguing by hospitals where the patient is restricted and personal connections had to be minimised. In order to mechanically transmit a meal tray to a table or furniture in the room, the robot acted as a powered conveyor. It is beneficial for patients, self-sufficient individuals, who need isolation during the COVID-19 pandemic [34, 35].

1.7 ROBOTICS APPLICATIONS FOR PUBLIC HEALTH AND SAFETY DURING THE COVID-19 PANDEMIC

Robotics improves the usage of medical facilities and reduce the danger of infection to humans who work there. There are many ordinary duties in medical institutions, most neglected and primarily entail infection exposure. Trash collection, room purification and disinfection of space, distribution of medicine and food supply are various activities done by robots to minimise the danger of medical staff. This also reduces the chance of one of the personnel becoming a patient themselves. Robotics can do various activities with the proper safeguards while preventing transmission between patients and staff. Autonomous, mobile robots are supported for secure vision and navigation to help in the COVID-19 crisis. Automation activities to limit exposure to human infection can allow the delivery of important services, increase security for frontline employees and enhance the efficiency of numerous services [36–38]. Table 1.2 discusses the significant applications of robotics for public health and safety during the COVID-19 pandemic.

Robotics is suitable for disinfecting and removing polluted facilities, not just in hospitals but also in schools, businesses and more. As time changes, this technology plays a part in fighting the COVID-19 pandemic. Robotics technology helps not only in supporting patients but also in keeping the doctor, healthcare and other personnel safe during the COVID-19 pandemic. These self-supporting services assist in retaining social distancing, allowing for less human interaction while delivering sensitive items of high quality and providing critical services [80–82]. This can deliver essential services to monitor and battle COVID-19 alone or with a public area technician. Intelligent safety systems can offer a crowd with temperature sensing. In many socioeconomic aspects, COVID-19 has altered the globe. The healthcare business is one of the most affected sectors. Apart from the humanitarian and health crises, medical personnel strive every day to keep people healthy and secure. Robotics has a key role in maintaining social distancing while helping patients and older people in care homes, and it also helps in maintaining health guidelines in hospitals [83–85].

1.8 DISCUSSION

The technological world is expanding and is having a significant effect on the future workplace. Robotics can be used to recognise any suspect actions as an intelligent machine. Several types of robots are helpful in measuring temperatures, cardiac rates and blood oxygen levels of admitted patients within the health centre. While the COVID-19 headlines are dominant, emergencies and options continue to be performed. Surgeons adjust their procedures to respond to the danger of infection, and robots offer a response in the theatre. The new generation of operating robotics can also save time for an operation, leading to fewer problems, shorter stays in hospitals and fewer receptions. The development and acceptance of robotic technology create innovation. This pandemic has transformed our social and medical risk relationship and has opened our minds to a technology that makes life simpler.

TABLE 1.2   Robotics Applications for Public Health and Safety during the COVID-19 Pandemic

S No	Applications	Description	References
1	Scan infected peoples	Robotic techniques are employed to scan for people with possible symptoms of the COVID-19 virus, rather than to risk employees at the admission site. It can have a significant influence in this regard. Mobile robots are utilised instead of physicians to conduct regular observations. They are used to deliver medications, which allows the nurses to help the patients in other ways. Robotics makes it possible for physicians and nurses to execute the highest priorities in healthcare.	[39–42]
2	Reduce transmission of the virus	One of the most important technologies to reduce the transmission of viruses is robots. There are already a considerable number of hospitals worldwide using robots that help both health workers and patients. It decreases the danger for both employees and patients substantially. This hazard to our friends and relatives can be significantly enhanced and eradicated by robotic aides. This technology played a crucial role in helping people to deal with present-day instances in the global struggle against COVID-19.	[43–45]
3	Assists patients	Robotics can assist patients to check at reception. It can help visitors to see whether there are any new viral symptoms. If a more complicated problem occurs, medical personnel may be consulted about the situation more accurately. It can decrease admissions to the hospital and help ensure that individuals have masks onsite using the checking option. This technology assists employees in ensuring that patients remain secure in the hospital and reduce the danger of interaction.	[46–48]
4	Meal delivery to COVID-19 patient	There is a danger in meal delivery in the isolated patient scenario. Thus, improvements are essential, given that they decrease the contact between health workers and the single patient. This technology is essential for the security of both the patients and the employees for reducing the spread of illness in the hospital. Medical professionals may be committed to the patients as much as possible. Robotics aids and do activities formerly carried out by their employees and may directly assist patients.	[49–51]
5	Enable social distancing	Patients in the struggle against the COVID-19 consider their safety and health as the top priority. Robots provide relief to the medical personnel by saving them thousands of rounds every day. This technology enables more social distancing, as the mobile robot may carry out transport in the hospital while medical personnel may stay at their working locations. Robots can safely pass through quarantine regions and clean up the areas making them ready for use without risking the safety of healthcare providers. Robots assist healthcare organisations, which are presently facing an outbreak, enhance their satisfactory.	[52–55]

(Continued)

TABLE 1.2 *(Continued)*   Robotics Applications for Public Health and Safety during the COVID-19 Pandemic

S No	Applications	Description	References
6	Scan temperature	A robot can make inquiries and can quickly scan the temperature of COVID-19 patients. Increasing automation after COVID-19 and changing workplaces will need more people, especially those with fewer qualifications, to look for new occupations. This issue can be easily resolved by using this technology. Robots have done a lot to combat COVID-19 and safeguard the frontline employees.	[56–58]
7	Convey information	The robot remains at the patient's bedside so that physicians may care for those who are actually ill. The robot watches the patient in the room and provides appropriate information to the hospital personnel. The patient can use the robot to record messages and speak with doctors. This helps to reduce the number of direct physicians and nurses with a patient considerably, therefore lowering the danger of infection.	[59–61]
8	Automating employment	The COVID-19 pandemic gives an incentive to automating employment in industries. The business will weigh the price of acquiring and maintaining a new machine or an artificial intelligence service system, labour expenses and other expenditures. Industries replace people with robots, whether automation is driven by a pandemic or by growing labour costs. This technology is helping countries to embrace the Fourth Industrial Revolution.	[62–65]
9	Healthcare Services	Within the area of delivery services, robotic applications are increasing. Amid the lockdown, several businesses and restaurants, on the one hand, and individuals at home, on the other hand, relied on home supplies. It allowed everything to be carried out contactless and became the safest approach. Standing in a line to pick up a pizza and supplying food to students on several university campuses. This allows for more automation than ever before. The drive for automation has been strengthened by increasing constraints on social gatherings.	[66–68]
10	Reduce human to human interaction	Robotics can decrease human-to-human interaction by scanning crowds and giving a warning when a person with excessive body temperature is sensed using the sensor in real-time. Robotics join forces to battle dangerous coronaviruses by building autonomous models exploring hospitals and other major installations. It also helps clean up areas and other surfaces where virus particles might spread among the affected population.	[69–72]

(Continued)

TABLE 1.2 (*Continued*)   Robotics Applications for Public Health and Safety during the
COVID-19 Pandemic

S No	Applications	Description	References
11	Medical advice	Some AI-enabled robots can even provide patients with medical advice and help in saving the time that health personnel have to invest. These robots are designed to aid healthcare experts to do daily duties. They can easily perform ultrasounds and listen to the organs of patients using a stethoscope. All these activities typically are easily carried out by individuals. This technology eliminates the need for humans to get in touch and may substantially limit the transmission of coronaviruses.	[73–75]
12	Telepresence	Telepresence robots frequently monitor the elderly and allow patients to speak with a doctor on the screen. In the course of the COVID-19 pandemic, telepresence robots help patients who are not permitted to go to intensive care centres. The robot may stand by the patient's bed and provide the facility of video conferencing using the tablet that it carries. These robots have also allowed doctors to remain in the house, do telemedicine and make them productive in emergency rooms while enabling nurses to view patients without worrying about personal protection. It is also utilised to improve patient monitoring, reaction times and healthcare, special needs and research support and enhance the safety of facilities.	[76–79]

COVID-19 increased the already onerous burden of health professionals throughout the world, but the additional fear has also arisen that healthcare personnel are infected through direct contact with patients. The emerging of medical robots in the field of biomedical engineering is becoming increasingly popular. They can work in many ways and different shapes. A remote-controlled, wheeled gadget with wireless Internet access is a telepresence robot. The incorporation of robots in healthcare has been discovered in various surgical operations to improve the accuracy, flexibility and control throughout the surgery. It is utilised to support medical workers in carrying out vital but possibly dangerous activities with the coronavirus. These are used to flag patients who had a fever, specific disease symptoms, need cardiac monitoring, have low oxygen levels and provide needed material to patient and healthcare workers at different locations.

1.9 CONCLUSION

The use of robotics technology considerably reduces the load of patients on the healthcare system and individuals under quarantine. Robotics also reduces the danger of the frontline employees being routinely exposed to the virus, and thus helps them in staying safe and making their most outstanding contributions in combating the COVID-19 pandemic. Robotics also uses their current autonomous platforms to work with patients and even provide medications within coronavirus wards. Automation and assembly are already in factories, but people also work with these robots and assist them. Prevention of diseases is essential in viral containment, and many times are done by disinfection and other methods. So, disinfection by robots is now utilised for reducing the virus spread over polluted or hazardous areas. Hospitals can use robots to decrease healthcare infections. Even for inpatient screening and diagnosis, robotics can also play an essential role and can serve as an important monitoring station. Robots did not replace human employment throughout the COVID-19 pandemic but made it safer and more efficient.

CONFLICT OF INTEREST

None.

REFERENCES

1. Tavakoli, M., Carriere, J., & Torabi, A. (2020). Robotics, smart wearable technologies, and autonomous intelligent systems for healthcare during the COVID-19 pandemic: An analysis of the state of the art and future vision. *Advanced Intelligent Systems*, *2*(7), 2000071.
2. Wu, S., Wu, D., Ye, R., Li, K., Lu, Y., Xu, J., & Lv, F. (2020). Pilot study of robot-assisted teleultrasound based on 5G network: A new feasible strategy for early imaging assessment during COVID-19 pandemic. *IEEE Transactions on Ultrasonics, Ferroelectrics, and Frequency Control*, *67*(11), 2241–2248.
3. Manjunatha, H., Pareek, S., Jujjavarapu, S. S., Ghobadi, M., Kesavadas, T., & Esfahani, E. T. (2021). Upper limb home-based robotic rehabilitation during COVID-19 outbreak. *Frontiers in Robotics and AI, 8*.
4. Thomas, M. J., Lal, V., Baby, A. K., James, A., & Raj, A. K. (2021). Can technological advancements help to alleviate COVID-19 pandemic? A review. *Journal of Biomedical Informatics, 117*, 103787.
5. Javaid, M., Haleem, A., Vaishya, R., Bahl, S., Suman, R., & Vaish A. (2020). Industry 4.0 technologies and their applications in fighting COVID-19 pandemic. *Diabetes & Metabolic Syndrome: Clinical Research & Reviews*, Jul 1; *14*(4), 419–422.
6. Cardona, M., Cortez, F., Palacios, A., & Cerros, K. (2020, October). Mobile Robots Application against Covid-19 Pandemic. In *2020 IEEE ANDESCON* (pp. 1–5). IEEE.
7. Ing, E. B., Xu, Q., Salimi, A., & Torun, N. (2020). Physician deaths from coronavirus (COVID-19) disease. *Occupational Medicine, 70*(5), 370–374.

8. Wang, X. V., & Wang, L. (2021). A literature survey of the robotic technologies during the COVID-19 pandemic. *Journal of Manufacturing Systems*, 70, 823–836.

9. Zeng, Z., Chen, P. J., & Lew, A. A. (2020). From high-touch to high-tech: COVID-19 drives robotics adoption. *Tourism Geographies*, *22*(3), 724–734.

10. Moschovas, M. C., Bhat, S., Rogers, T., Onol, F., Roof, S., Sighinolfi, M. C., … Patel, V. (2021). Managing patients with prostate cancer during COVID-19 pandemic: The experience of a high-volume robotic surgery center. *Journal of Endourology*, *35*(3), 305–311.

11. Isabet, B., Pino, M., Lewis, M., Benveniste, S., & Rigaud, A. S. (2021). Social telepresence robots: A narrative review of experiments involving older adults before and during the COVID-19 pandemic. *International Journal of Environmental Research and Public Health*, *18*(7), 3597.

12. Di Lallo, A., Murphy, R., Krieger, A., Zhu, J., Taylor, R. H., & Su, H. (2021). Medical robots for infectious diseases: Lessons and challenges from the COVID-19 pandemic. *IEEE Robotics & Automation Magazine*, *28*(1), 18–27.

13. Kimmig, R., Verheijen, R. H., & Rudnicki, M. (2020). Robot-assisted surgery during the COVID-19 pandemic, especially for gynecological cancer: A statement of the Society of European Robotic Gynaecological Surgery (SERGS). *Journal of Gynecologic Oncology*, *31*(3), e59.

14. Yang, G., Lv, H., Zhang, Z., Yang, L., Deng, J., You, S., … & Yang, H. (2020). Keep healthcare workers safe: Application of teleoperated robot in isolation ward for COVID-19 prevention and control. *Chinese Journal of Mechanical Engineering*, *33*(1), 1–4.

15. Sierra Marín, S. D., Gomez-Vargas, D., Céspedes, N., Múnera, M., Roberti, F., Barria, P., … Cifuentes, C. A. (2021). Expectations and perceptions of healthcare professionals for robot deployment in hospital environments during the COVID-19 pandemic. *Frontiers in Robotics and AI*, 8, 102.

16. Chen, B., Marvin, S., & While, A. (2020). Containing COVID-19 in China: AI and the robotic restructuring of future cities. *Dialogues in Human Geography*, *10*(2), 238–241.

17. Ashima, R., Haleem, A., Bahl, S., Javaid, M., Mahla, SK., & Singh, S. (2021). Automation and manufacturing of smart materials in Additive Manufacturing technologies using Internet of Things towards the adoption of Industry 4.0. *Materials Today: Proceedings*, Jan 1; 45, 5081–5088.

18. Khan, H., Kushwah, K. K., Singh, S., Urkude, H., Maurya, M. R., & Sadasivuni, K. K. (2021). Smart technologies driven approaches to tackle COVID-19 pandemic: A review. *3 Biotech*, *11*(2), 1–22.

19. Feizi, N., Tavakoli, M., Patel, R. V., & Atashzar, S. F. (2021). Robotics and AI for teleoperation, tele-assessment, and tele-training for surgery in the era of covid-19: Existing challenges, and future vision. *Frontiers in Robotics and AI*, 8, 610677.

20. Kaiser, M. S., Al Mamun, S., Mahmud, M., & Tania, M. H. (2021). Healthcare robots to combat COVID-19. In *COVID-19: Prediction, Decision-Making, and Its Impacts* (pp. 83–97). Springer, Singapore.

21. Atashzar, S. F., Carriere, J., & Tavakoli, M. (2021). How can intelligent robots and smart mechatronic modules facilitate remote assessment, assistance, and rehabilitation for isolated adults with neuro-musculoskeletal conditions?. *Frontiers in Robotics and AI, 8*. 610529

22. Joshi, S., Collins, S., Kamino, W., Gomez, R., & Šabanović, S. (2020, November). Social Robots for Socio-Physical Distancing. In *International Conference on Social Robotics* (pp. 440–452). Springer, Cham.

23. Vicente, R., Mohamed, Y., Eguíluz, V. M., Zemmar, E., Bayer, P., Neimat, J. S., … Zemmar, A. (2021). Modelling the impact of robotics on infectious spread among healthcare workers. *Frontiers in Robotics and AI, 8*. 652685.

24. Gittens, C. (2021, January). Remote-HRI: A pilot study to evaluate a methodology for performing HRI research during the COVID-19 pandemic. In *Proceedings of the 54th Hawaii International Conference on System Sciences* (p. 1878).

25. Tsoi, N., Connolly, J., Adéníran, E., Hansen, A., Pineda, K. T., Adamson, T., … Scassellati, B. (2021, March). Challenges deploying robots during a pandemic: An effort to fight social isolation among children. In *Proceedings of the 2021 ACM/IEEE International Conference on Human-Robot Interaction* (pp. 234–242).

26. Yoshikawa, Y., Kumazaki, H., & Kato, T. A. (2021). Future perspectives of robot psychiatry: Can communication robots assist psychiatric evaluation in the COVID-19 pandemic era?. *Current Opinion in Psychiatry, 34*(3), 277–286.

27. Nasajpour, M., Pouriyeh, S., Parizi, R. M., Dorodchi, M., Valero, M., & Arabnia, H. R. (2020). Internet of Things for current COVID-19 and future pandemics: An exploratory study. *Journal of Healthcare Informatics Research*, 1–40.

28. Somashekhar, S. P., Acharya, R., Manjiri, S., Talwar, S., Ashwin, K. R., & Rohit Kumar, C. (2020). Adaptations and safety modifications to perform safe minimal access surgery (Minimally Invasive Surgery: Laparoscopy and Robotic) during the COVID-19 pandemic. *Surgical Innovation*, 1553350620964323.

29. Gao, A., Murphy, R. R., Chen, W., Dagnino, G., Fischer, P., Gutierrez, M. G., … Yang, G. Z. (2021). Progress in robotics for combating infectious diseases. *Science Robotics, 6*(52).

30. Li, C., Gu, X., Xiao, X., Lim, C. M., Duan, X., & Ren, H. (2021). A flexible transoral robot towards COVID-19 swab sampling. *Frontiers in Robotics and AI, 8*, 51.

31. Jiang, Y., & Wen, J. (2020). Effects of COVID-19 on hotel marketing and management: a perspective article. *International Journal of Contemporary Hospitality Management*.

32. Vafea, M. T., Atalla, E., Georgakas, J., Shehadeh, F., Mylona, E. K., Kalligeros, M., & Mylonakis, E. (2020). Emerging technologies for use in the study, diagnosis, and treatment of patients with COVID-19. *Cellular and Molecular Bioengineering, 13*(4), 249–257.

33. Jovanovic, K., Schwier, A., Matheson, E., Xiloyannis, M., Rozeboom, E., Hochhausen, N., … Stramigioli, S. (2021). Digital innovation hubs in health-care robotics fighting COVID-19: Novel support for patients and health-care workers across Europe. *IEEE Robotics & Automation Magazine*, *28*(1), 40–47.

34. Seidita, V., Lanza, F., Pipitone, A., & Chella, A. (2021). Robots as intelligent assistants to face COVID-19 pandemic. *Briefings in Bioinformatics*, *22*(2), 823–831.

35. Virk, H. U. H., Lakhter, V., Tabaza, L., & George, J. C. (2020). Do we need robotics for coronary intervention more than ever in the COVID-19 era? *Catheterisation and Cardiovascular Interventions*.

36. Kulpa, E., Rahman, A. T., & Vahia, I. V. (2021). Approaches to assessing the impact of robotics in geriatric mental health care: A scoping review. *International Review of Psychiatry*, *33*, 1–11.

37. Khan, Z. H., Siddique, A., & Lee, C. W. (2020). Robotics utilisation for healthcare digitisation in global COVID-19 management. *International Journal of Environmental Research and Public Health*, *17*(11), 3819.

38. Hussain, K., Wang, X., Omar, Z., Elnour, M., & Ming, Y. (2021, January). Robotics and Artificial Intelligence Applications in Manage and Control of COVID-19 Pandemic. In *2021 International Conference on Computer, Control and Robotics (ICCCR)* (pp. 66–69). IEEE.

39. Bačík, J., Tkáč, P., Hric, L., Alexovič, S., Kyslan, K., Olexa, R., & Perduková, D. (2020). Phollower—The universal autonomous mobile robot for industry and civil environments with COVID-19 germicide addon meeting safety requirements. *Applied Sciences*, *10*(21), 7682.

40. Jain, R., Gupta, M., Garg, K., & Gupta, A. (2021). Robotics and drone-based solution for the impact of COVID-19 worldwide using AI and IoT. *Emerging Technologies for Battling Covid-19: Applications and Innovations*, 139–156.

41. Javaid, M., & Haleem, A. (2019). Industry 4.0 applications in medical field: A brief review. *Current Medicine Research and Practice*, May 1; *9*(3), 102–109.

42. Alsamhi, S. H., & Lee, B. (2020). Blockchain-empowered Multi-robot collaboration to fight COVID-19 and future pandemics. *IEEE Access*, *9*, 44173–44197.

43. El Khatib, M., Al Falasi, H., Al Moosawi, M., & Shafi, S. B. (2021). The role of robotics in mitigating unknown-unknown risks: Case of COVID-19. *Journal of Service Science and Management*, *14*(01), 1.

44. Khamis, A., Meng, J., Wang, J., Azar, A. T., Prestes, E., Li, H., … Haidegger, T. (2021). Robotics and intelligent systems against a pandemic. *Acta Polytechnica Hungarica*, *18*(5).

45. Ahmed, S. N. (2021). Covid, AI, and robotics—A neurologist's perspective. *Frontiers in Robotics and AI*, *8*, 73.

46. Scott, B. K., Miller, G. T., Fonda, S. J., Yeaw, R. E., Gaudaen, J. C., Pavliscsak, H. H., … Pamplin, J. C. (2020). Advanced digital health technologies for COVID-19 and future emergencies. *Telemedicine and e-Health*, *26*(10), 1226–1233.

47. Ñope-Giraldo, R. M., Illapuma-Ccallo, L. A., Cornejo, J., Palacios, P., Napán, J. L., Cruz, F., … Vargas, M. (2021, March). Mechatronic Systems Design of ROHNI-1: Hybrid Cyber-Human Medical Robot for COVID-19 Health Surveillance at Wholesale-Supermarket Entrances. In *2021 Global Medical Engineering Physics Exchanges/Pan American Health Care Exchanges (GMEPE/PAHCE)* (pp. 1–7). IEEE.

48. Ammar, M., Haleem, A., Javaid, M., Walia, R., & Bahl, S. (2021). Improving material quality management and manufacturing organisations system through Industry 4.0 technologies. *Materials Today: Proceedings*, Jan 1; *45*, 5089–5096.

49. Abhishek, K., Dalla, V. K., & Shrivastava, A. (2021, May). Humanoid robot applications in COVID-19: A comprehensive study. In *AIP Conference Proceedings* (Vol. 2341, No. 1, p. 020040). AIP Publishing LLC.

50. Houacine, N. A., & Drias, H. (2021). When robots contribute to eradicate the COVID-19 spread in a context of containment. *Progress in Artificial Intelligence*, 1–26.

51. Joshi, P., Tyagi, R. K., & Agarwal, K. M. (2021). Technological resources for fighting COVID-19 pandemic health issues. *Journal of Industrial Integration and Management*, *6*(02), 271–285.

52. Le, A. V., Ramalingam, B., Gómez, B. F., Mohan, R. E., Minh, T. H. Q., & Sivanantham, V. (2021). Social density monitoring toward selective cleaning by human support robot with 3D based perception system. *IEEE Access*, *9*, 41407–41416.

53. Minor, K., McLoughlin, E., & Richards, V. (2021). Enhancing the visitor experience in the time of COVID 19: The use of AI robotics in Pembrokeshire Coastal Pathway. In *Information and Communication Technologies in Tourism 2021* (pp. 570–577). Springer, Cham.

54. Zaroushani, V., & Khajehnesiri, F. (2020). Nurse robots: A necessity in the nursing care system during the Covid-19 pandemic. *Journal of Occupational Health and Epidemiology*, *9*(3), 130–132.

55. Singh, S., Dalla, V. K., & Shrivastava, A. (2021, May). Combating COVID-19: Study of robotic solutions for COVID-19. In *AIP Conference Proceedings* (Vol. 2341, No. 1, p. 020042). AIP Publishing LLC.

56. Firouzi, F., Farahani, B., Daneshmand, M., Grise, K., Song, J. S., Saracco, R., … Luo, A. (2021). Harnessing the power of smart and connected health to tackle COVID-19: IoT, AI, robotics, and blockchain for a better world. *IEEE Internet of Things Journal*.

57. Tamantini, C., di Luzio, F. S., Cordella, F., Pascarella, G., Agro, F. E., & Zollo, L. (2021). A Robotic health-care assistant for COVID-19 emergency: A proposed solution for logistics and disinfection in a hospital environment. *IEEE Robotics & Automation Magazine*, *28*(1), 71–81.

58. Bhaskar, S., Bradley, S., Sakhamuri, S., Moguilner, S., Chattu, V. K., Pandya, S., … Banach, M. (2020). Designing futuristic telemedicine using artificial intelligence and robotics in the COVID-19 era. *Frontiers in Public Health*, *8*, 708.

59. Wang, S., Wang, K., Tang, R., Qiao, J., Liu, H., & Hou, Z. G. (2020). Design of a low-cost miniature robot to assist the COVID-19 nasopharyngeal swab sampling. *IEEE Transactions on Medical Robotics and Bionics.*

60. Gupta, A., Singh, A., Bharadwaj, D., & Mondal, A. K. (2021). Humans and robots: A mutually inclusive relationship in a contagious world. *International Journal of Automation and Computing,* 1–19.

61. Musanabaganwa, C., Semakula, M., Mazarati, J. B., Nyamusore, J., Uwimana, A., Kayumba, M., … Nsanzimana, S. (2020). Use of technologies in Covid-19 containment in Rwanda. *Rwanda Public Health Bulletin, 2*(2), 7–12.

62. Clipper, B. (2020). The influence of the COVID-19 pandemic on technology: adoption in health care. *Nurse Leader, 18*(5), 500–503.

63. Caselli, M., Fracasso, A., & Traverso, S. (2020). Mitigation of risks of Covid-19 contagion and robotisation: evidence from Italy. *Covid Economics, 17,* 174–188.

64. Mohanty, K., Subiksha, S., Kirthika, S., Sujal, B. H., Sokkanarayanan, S., Bose, P., & Sathiyanarayanan, M. (2021, January). Opportunities of Adopting AI-Powered Robotics to Tackle COVID-19. In *2021 International Conference on COMmunication Systems & NETworkS (COMSNETS)* (pp. 703–708). IEEE.

65. Malik, A. A., Masood, T., & Kousar, R. (2020). Repurposing factories with robotics in the face of COVID-19. *Science Robotics, 5*(43).

66. Marchetti, A., Di Dio, C., Massaro, D., & Manzi, F. (2020). The psychosocial fuzziness of fear in the coronavirus (COVID-19) era and the role of robots. *Frontiers in Psychology, 11,* 2245.

67. Henkel, A. P., Čaić, M., Blaurock, M., & Okan, M. (2020). Robotic transformative service research: deploying social robots for consumer well-being during Covid-19 and beyond. *Journal of Service Management.*

68. Porter, J. R., Blau, E., Gharagozloo, F., Martino, M., Cerfolio, R., Duvvuri, U., … Patel, V. (2020). Society of Robotic Surgery review: Recommendations regarding the risk of COVID-19 transmission during minimally invasive surgery. *BJU International, 126*(2), 225.

69. Chai, P. R., Dadabhoy, F. Z., Huang, H. W., Chu, J. N., Feng, A., Le, H. M., … & Traverso, G. (2021). Assessment of the acceptability and feasibility of using mobile robotic systems for patient evaluation. *JAMA Network Open, 4*(3), e210667–e210667.

70. Blanc, T., Pinar, U., Anract, J., Assouad, J., Audenet, F., Borghese, B., … Roupret, M. (2021). Impact of the COVID-19 pandemic on oncological and functional robotic-assisted surgical procedures. *Journal of Robotic Surgery,* 1–8.

71. Guettari, M., Gharbi, I., & Hamza, S. (2020). UVC disinfection robot. *Environmental Science and Pollution Research,* 1–6.

72. Mazzoleni, S., Turchetti, G., & Ambrosino, N. (2020). The COVID-19 outbreak: From "black swan" to global challenges and opportunities. *Pulmonology, 26*(3), 117.

73. Cooper, S., Di Fava, A., Vivas, C., Marchionni, L., & Ferro, F. (2020, August). ARI: the Social Assistive Robot and Companion. In *2020 29th IEEE International Conference on Robot and Human Interactive Communication (RO-MAN)* (pp. 745–751). IEEE.

74. Asadzadeh, A., Pakkhoo, S., Saeidabad, M. M., Khezri, H., & Ferdousi, R. (2020). Information technology in emergency management of COVID-19 outbreak. *Informatics in Medicine Unlocked*, 100475.

75. Cresswell, K., Ramalingam, S., & Sheikh, A. (2020). Can robots improve testing capacity for SARS-CoV-2?. *Journal of Medical Internet research*, 22(8), e20169.

76. Michaud, F., Boissy, P., Labonte, D., Corriveau, H., Grant, A., Lauria, M., ... Royer, MP. (2007). Telepresence robot for home care assistance. In *AAAI Spring Symposium: Multidisciplinary Collaboration for Socially Assistive Robotics* Mar 26 (pp. 50–55).

77. Javaid, M., Haleem, A., Singh, RP., & Suman, R. (2021). Substantial capabilities of robotics in enhancing industry 4.0 implementation. *Cognitive Robotics.* Jun 6.

78. Zampolli, H. C., & Rodriguez, A. R. (2020). Laparoscopic and robotic urology surgery during global Pandemic COVID-19. *International Brazilian Journal of Urology*, 46, 215–221.

79. Zemmar, A., Lozano, A. M., & Nelson, B. J. (2020). The rise of robots in surgical environments during COVID-19. *Nature Machine Intelligence*, 2(10), 566–572.

80. Javaid, M., Haleem, A., Vaish, A., Vaishya, R., & Iyengar KP. (2020). Robotics applications in COVID-19: A review. *Journal of Industrial Integration and Management*, 5(4).

81. Abdel-Basset, M., Chang, V., & Nabeeh, N. A. (2021). An intelligent framework using disruptive technologies for COVID-19 analysis. *Technological Forecasting and Social Change*, 163, 120431.

82. Dai, X., Li, H., & Ning, M. (2021). Plasma robot engineering: The next generation of precision disease management. *Annals of Biomedical Engineering*, 1–5.

83. Chamola, V., Hassija, V., Gupta, V., & Guizani, M. (2020). A comprehensive review of the COVID-19 pandemic and the role of IoT, drones, AI, blockchain, and 5G in managing its impact. *IEEE Access*, 8, 90225–90265.

84. Teng, X., Teng, Y. M., Wu, K. S., & Chang, B. G. (2021). Corporate social responsibility in public health during the COVID-19 pandemic: quarantine hotel in China. *Frontiers in Public Health*, 9.

85. Lemos, P. A., Franken, M., Mariani Jr, J., Pitta, F. G., Oliveira, F. A., Cunha-Lima, G., & Garcia, R. G. (2020). Robotic-assisted intervention strategy to minimise air exposure during the procedure: A case report of myocardial infarction and COVID-19. *Cardiovascular Diagnosis and Therapy*, 10(5), 1345.

CHAPTER 2

Beauty in Interaction

A Framework for Social Robot Aesthetics (Pandemic Edition)

Rebekah Rousi

School of Marketing and Communication, University of Vaasa, Vaasa, Finland

Gofore Plc, Tampere, Finland

Sini Kolari

Faculty of Information Technology, University of Jyväskylä, Jyväskylä, Finland

Mohammad Shidujaman

Department of Art and Design, Tsinghua University, Beijing, China

CONTENTS

DOI: 10.1201/9781003195061-2

2.1 INTRODUCTION

Throughout history, humans have been fascinated in creating their likeness. Evidence can be seen through centuries' worth of popular culture, philosophy and science alike. Whether it has been a question of creating a friend, lover, child or servant, machine-based human likenesses have never failed to capture human attention and the imagination. Moreover, it is not simply the machines that resemble humans in some way that trigger humans to deal with machine objects as if they were human. For instance, in their book *The Man Who Lied to His Laptop: What We Can Learn about Ourselves from Our Machines*, Clifford Nass and Corina Yen [1] presented research that demonstrates how people can feel equally as much for machines as they can for other people. Nass and Yen focused on anthropomorphism – the way in which humans treat objects like people (able to experience emotions and feel). In particular, their work highlights how mechanically animated objects and information technology (IT) generate responses in humans, which make them instinctively feel that these objects have a mind (cognition) and indeed soul (experiential consciousness) of their own.

A range of emotions were shown to arise through social interaction with the computers. In Nass and Yen's reported studies, different types of linguistic responses to study participants generated various types of emotions and attitudes towards the computers. Empathy, in particular, was one of the forms of emotional responses that arose in situations where the computer was not behaving (operating) in the way it should have, yet experiment subjects were 'kind' to the computer in order to avoid hurting its feelings. This approach to animated technology can be viewed and explained from a number of ways, none-the-least one in which humans resist insulting the technology in fear that it will get offended and, in turn, will malfunction in retaliation. Thus, through anthropomorphism a form of cybernetic (organic combined with non-organic) intersubjectivity, or the sharing of experience [2], can be observed. This intersubjectivity serves to predict and adjust to the behaviours and reactions of the other interactive party [3] and anticipate or expect the behavioural reactions in return [4]. Thus, people modify their behaviour in anticipation of the capabilities and reactive behaviour of the other parties in any interactional situation [5].

Not only does this example give insight into the ways in which humans automatically endow objects with emotions and consciousness, but it also highlights the complexity of social interaction. This social interaction is a dynamic, transactional process in which numerous factors are at play, informing the experience of the interaction itself and its aesthetic qualities [6]. In the realm of human-computer interaction (HCI) much attention has been placed on aesthetics as a means of defining attractiveness or beauty as opposed to unattractiveness or ugliness [7]. Philosophical traditions in aesthetics, however, show that aesthetics and these perceptions of the qualities of aesthetic experience are not so easily classified or opposed to one another [8].

In the year 2021, it is little surprising that ever increasing attention is being drawn towards the design and development of intelligent systems. Coupled with this development of the previously imagined possibility of autonomously functioning and learning machines is naturally the excitement of the possibilities for our mechanical friends to be realised. By mechanical friends, we refer to artificial companions – robots – who can communicate, think and enable humans to feel as though they were engaged in meaningful social interaction, generating social experiences of a genuine nature [9]. Much of the research to this end has focused on human perceptions and emotional reactions to robot design from a visual perspective (see e.g. [10]).

2.1.1 Why Social Robots? Basic Needs and Human Social Make Up

The COVID-19 pandemic has shed light on numerous complex problems – both economic and biological. The social needs of human beings can be seen as closely linked to human biological and psychological make up [11]. Healthy, active social relationships and interactions can be seen to inspire thought and motivate humans towards engaging in action, whether it be learning or creating (from building a house to cooking or designing) [12]. In fact, aesthetic experience can be seen as the act of doing, making sense of the world through the body, its positioning and interactions [13–15]. These basic building blocks can be understood as constantly present in social interaction – encouraging or discouraging humans from engaging in interaction.

Social interactions and relationships in themselves are manifold. The variation in these types of interactions and relations also means a diverse range of compositions of how and what we are experiencing. Interactions not only comprise two or more individuals, but also context, purpose, intention, motivation, etc. The social isolation caused by social distancing during the COVID-19 pandemic has placed substantial limits on the range of social interactions people can experience with others. While people have sought alternative avenues for social contact from increased video conferencing to deeper engagement in social media and overall Internet content, the matter of these media being insufficient for compensating real physical contact and proximity is an issue that is constantly raised (see e.g. [16, 17]). The limitations of physical social contact raise questions regarding social well-being. While the construct of social well-being in itself needs to be carefully deconstructed and analysed, the interactional and relational experience involved in contributing to, or deteriorating, this social well-being should also be understood. For this reason, here we focus on the aesthetics of social robot design to isolate the experiential properties involved in human social robot interaction [18].

In order to approach this topic, we consider five dimensions to begin with: (1) the *why*, (2) the *variables*, (3) the *how*, (4) the *assessment* of resources and (5) the *what*. Before embarking on the commitment to design social robotics, there needs to be an understanding of the *why* – why venture into the topic of social robotic design in the first place? What is there to achieve from the interaction itself? Then, there are the *variables* – what are the factors involved that affect the experience of social interactions in various use contexts? Given the situation much faced by the members of the global population during lockdown, the reality of existing in a small apartment without physical human social contact, it is important to understand what from human lived experience remains and what is missing when not engaged in physical social contact. Moreover, and of great importance to this chapter, are the exact factors aesthetically (physically), socially and psychologically that are at play when engaged in social interaction with robots. The composites of these factors can be divided into:

- The environment (where interaction happens)
- The actors/agents (with whom/what? And the factors/associations connected to these actors/agents)
- Mental and physical states of the human(s)
- Material design and logic of the robot

When deliberating on the concrete levels of design, system logic and development, it is also important to understand which variables are somewhat consistent in social aesthetic experience, and what may be dynamic and altering. Thus, the *how* is critical when attempting to match human–robot interactive experience to context. That is, how should the variables change in order to reach the intended end result (desired experiential outcome)? Additionally, from this perspective we may pose the query of the degree to which we, as designers or engineers, can affect and/or control the variables contributing to the aesthetic experience of social interaction with robots.

An assessment of *resources* (both immaterial and materials factors) should be undertaken to know what is at hand in terms of designing for social experience. This leads to the *what*, of determining the technical (functionalities) and aesthetic design choices (physical attributes) that should be made for the systems in relation to their possible use contexts, and the variation between use contexts. Indeed, there should be an evaluation of whether or not the desired end result can be achieved through the assistance of robotics after all, or whether there would be another way of achieving an even better social experiential result (for instance, alternatives may be virtual or augmented reality, multisensory internet or even reading poetry and consuming other cultural products, etc.).

2.2 SOCIOLOGICAL DIMENSIONS OF SOCIAL INTERACTION

Social interaction, or social relations, describes the connection or relationship involving two or more people [55]. Social interaction often involves speech or written communication, yet not always. Social interaction may involve body language and other communicative or action cues. Communication in itself can be seen as one of the fundamental bases of society [19]. In interactions or relationships, verbal or natural linguistic communication may or may not take place, yet there is some kind of interaction or processing of the other's presence and features, and what these mean to each perceiver from an individual standpoint [20]. Individual agency is therefore a fundamental component of social interactions as it establishes a platform upon which social structure is formed. In relation to sociologist Max Weber's [21] social action theory, a social act is a behaviour that accounts for the behaviour (actions) and reactions (responses) or individuals (agents). Here, actions and behaviour are social if they are aimed towards and considered in relation to other agents. Thus, when subjective meaning is attributed to others and in conjunction with behaviour connected with others, it is considered social.

While the above describes social interaction in a nutshell, this is indeed an oversimplification of Weber's theory of social action. In fact, it seems that Weber [22] likens action to a simple gesture or movement within a specific environment or context [11]. It becomes a social action when it is purposefully and meaningfully aimed towards others [11, 22]. Weber organised social actions into three main types: 1) rational – instrumental-rational (calculated and strategic) and value-rational (creation of moral standards); 2) affectual – actions implicated with emotions and feelings; and 3) traditional – social actions that are guided by habit and custom. The types link social actions from micro (individual) levels to macro (community and societal) levels and vice versa.

Likewise, Talcott Parsons [23] connected the micro to the macro level in his adapted model of social action. Parsons was influenced by intellectual traditions that included positivism, utilitarianism and idealism and had placed a considerable amount of work into explaining human behaviour in terms of unit acts that are said to be guided by norms, beliefs and various symbols. Parsons argued that humans were limited by their own ideas and material realities [11]. This links the individual level actions defined by both the psycho-biological circumstances of the actor (human) to the ecology of their situation. Quite readily, during the current COVID-19 pandemic, this relationship can be understood through the biology of prevention (social distancing to reduce spread of the viral infection), and psycho-biology of the reality of this social distancing – the conditions individuals live in within their limited face-to-face social contact, and how this in turn affects physical contact when restrictions are lessened.

Also, as is experienced and known in the current global conditions of crisis, social systems and the systems associated with social interactions are complex. In his book *The Structure of Social Action* Parsons [23] states, 'any atomistic system that deals only with the properties identifiable in the unit act ... will of necessity fail to treat these latter elements adequately and be indeterminate as applied to complex systems' (p. 748–49). This is an important point to remember from the perspective of designing social robots and robotics for social interaction, as the micro, or unit-based perspective, fails to account for the multi-dimensionality, dynamics and variation of social interactions and experiences within these complex systems – the connected world of data, as well as human systems in the world at large. Parsons' terminology of action refers to orientations that are linked to either motivation or value. *Interaction*, rather than pure action, comes into play when individual actors need to reconcile their orientations – i.e. there is a rebound, reflection and/or reciprocation of the actions and their orientations in relation to other actors[1].

2.2.1 Social Systems

Thus, social interactions derive when actions are targeted towards other actors, and these in turn are reciprocated and reconciled [11]. This can be understood equally in relation to humans' actions towards other humans, as in terms of interactions with technological artefacts, services and systems [55]. Social systems emerge and evolve when interactions become formalised and systematically repeated. Parsons [23] argued that social systems could be classified and categorised. These classifications are referred to as pattern variables, also known in the work of Weber as 'social relations' and 'legitimated orders'.

These social systems can be seen to represent macro processes characterised by binaries that entail: universalism versus particularism; achievement versus ascription; neutrality versus affectivity. Moving down Parsons' model towards the micro, we can see these social systems emerging through the institutionalisation of interaction, that in turn are characterised by interaction that form our understanding of actions as instrumental, expressive and moral. According to Parsons, social systems can be deconstructed into units. These units inform modes of orientation that are divided into motivational factors (cognitive, cathectic, evaluative) and value-based factors (cognitive, appreciative, moral). These form the nature of interactions, or indeed actions, derived at the micro level. Parsons' model has received substantial critique. Namely Jonathan Turner criticised Parsons theoretical model for its inadequacies in analysing micro processes. That is, these micro level, or individual level, factors and processes that are present and activated in interaction were not seen by Turner to be properly accounted for. Moreover, Turner argued that any static typology that aims to explain interaction and its properties will fall short of affording access to factors that contribute to interactions, their circumstances and experiences. There is also contention about the movement between understandings of micro and macro processes, and particularly the attention that is drawn to this movement before enough understanding has been drawn from either [11]. An outcome of this type of treatment of social interactions can be seen in heavily laden metaphorical assertions that macro processes are simply micro processes on different scales [26, 27] and/or micro are macro processes at the individual level [28].

2.2.2 Symbolic Interactionism

From sociology to psychology (social, behaviourist and phenomenological), including symbolic interactionism [26], crucial attention is claimed to be needed in terms of understanding the interaction between symbolic or outer, expressive elements of interaction and communication with inner mechanisms. Symbolic interactionism for instance is claimed by Blumer to observe the way in which one's concept of world is shaped in interaction with others – others, including these expressive, symbolic elements. In fact, as a method for symbolically interpreting and analysing social interactions, symbolic interactionism describes how we connect to and navigate our world through series, networks and spaces of symbols [29–31]. In fact, symbolic interactionism was one of the main trajectories of semiotics (the science of signs) and pragmatism as we know it today (see e.g. [31, 32]) whereby the human mind is in constant symbolic interaction with the world through signs [33, 34]. What is more, these signs are relevant for communicating to individuals cognitively and affectively about the relationship they as humans have regarding the interactive phenomena with which they are encountering.

This process constantly places the self (I, the personal self; or me the ecological contextualised self) in a comparative and evaluative relationship towards the *other* (person, technological design, animal, environment, etc.) [26]. Equally, from a cognitive-affective perspective, similar observations are made in evolutionary psychology, particularly in the theories of Appraisal [35–37] and Core Affect [38, 39] emotions emerge in relation to how people evaluate phenomena against what the phenomena can do in terms of promoting or affecting their primary concern – psychophysiological well-being (of the body).

Thus, social interactions, and being in the world through spaces of symbolic interactions positioning and affecting the *I* or *me* in relation to the *other*, also induce primary emotional reactions (i.e. basic emotions such as fear, disgust, anger) – those which are immediate to humans in reaction to particular circumstances – as well as higher level or higher order emotional reactions that take place cognitively and associatively [40, 41]. In Turner's opinion, within social interaction individuals seek the need for trust and self-confirmation. There is also the need for reduction in anxiety – anxiety being generated by the unknown, or likelihood of something posing harm to their wellbeing. Humans are dispositioned to seek group and community inclusion, in addition to the symbolic material gratification of the *I* [11]. There is a direct effect between group inclusion and acceptance by others on gratification and reduction in anxiety. Thus, the role of symbolism in identification, group coherence and interactional synergy cannot be underplayed, as the designs and expressions of these symbols and their application send conscious and subconscious messages in interaction that convey not simply discursive messages, but also emotional ones [42, 43]. The experience of belonging to a group or within a relationship is affected by people's ability to receive symbolic (discursive) and material rewards that are implicated as a continual component of interaction.

2.3 SOCIAL INTERACTION AND ASSEMBLAGES

Everything and everyone exists in contexts, which in turn exist in systems. Thus, when referring to complex systems, it must be remembered that the intelligent technological artefacts themselves are not the only phenomena presenting complexity, but rather, so too do the human systems surrounding them (social, cultural, political, economic, etc.). We may think of these systems as networks, and in the same fashion as we turned to sociology for our understanding of social interaction above, we will once more turn to sociology, yet this time in our description of Actor Network Theory (ANT) [44], and particularly assemblages. ANT provides value for explaining the aesthetics of social interaction, and especially social robot design, as it exemplifies the dynamics and characteristics of the layers of our soon to be presented framework for social robot aesthetics (SoRAes) in action.

ANT is a theory that strives to explain the natural, synthetic and social world humans exist in [44]. It is a social theory that puts forward the idea that social forces are not self-contained units. Rather, social phenomena and interactions should be dealt with empirically to describe, not explain, how social activity has operated in certain circumstances [44]. This form of argumentation would also, to a degree, cancel any attempts to construct a firm aesthetic model for social robot design, due to the fact that all social interactional processes are constantly in flux. Yet, from a human–robot social interactional perspective, ANT is ideal for understanding the social activities, relationships and dynamics between humans and nonhumans, as all actors (people and objects) within the network are equal.

Then, if we move deeper into ANT and in particular observe Assemblage Theory (AT) we can understand that all objects, people and contexts exist in assemblages – systems of other actors (components) that formulate together in particular ways to give meaning, shape experience and formulate action [45]. While one may be tempted to think of these assemblages as clusters, they are rather multidimensional and layered compositions of elements and factors that shape the existence of phenomena. For instance, the design and object of a stirrup means nothing on its own. Rather, the stirrup gains meaning and takes shape through its combination with a horse and its rider [46]. The experience and existence of this assemblage is in turn affected by context and the addition of other objects, i.e. rifle, military uniform, or show grooming, etc. The stirrup is but one component in a systemic object, composition – assemblage. The addition of context, its factors (material conditions, objects, etc.), actors (onlookers and affectors), changes the coding of the overall assemblage in terms of how it is interpreted and operates. A similar type of logic exists within AT as can be seen in for instance in Daniel Dennett's (2006) 'Framing Problem' in AI programming, whereby each actor or element within a context contributes to a different set of possible events, and every piece of information could result in a different *narrative* or sequence of thoughts.

This holds for AT from a social actor perspective. Deleuze and Guattari [45] argued that material and linguistic systems are self-organised through means of territorialisation (stabilisation of the components of an assemblage through homogenisation of its components or the appropriation of

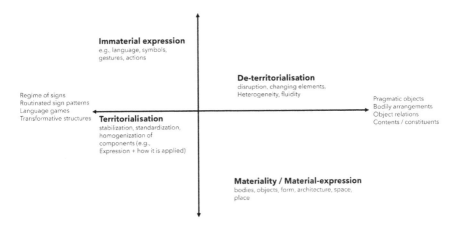

FIGURE 2.1 Social assemblages adapted from DeLanda's [46] map of exteriorised relations.

components from a homogenised source, e.g. routines, rituals, gestures specialised vocabulary), stratification or strata (social wholes) and coding (linguistic function of fixing identities of the strata). Manuel DeLanda [46, 47] systematically explains AT in a way that has often been referred to in the fields of design. In Delanda's account, there are series of specific functions that are shared among assemblages. Similar to Deleuze and Guattari, these are the material-expressive; territorialisation-deterritorialisation; and coding-decoding (see Figure 2.1). DeLanda explains that there are great variations in assemblage components that play a material-expressive role. Yet, the minimum requirement of these material components is that they feature sets of human bodies that are psychologically and physically oriented in relation to one another. From a semiotic (sign-system) perspective, this enables the social-interpretive element in which intentionality shapes material expression (coding), and equally, intentionality and cognitive-affective human processing serves to interpret (de-code) the expression [48]. A simple example of this type of assemblage is a face-to-face conversation. Drawing on both Parsons and Weber's models of social action and interaction, we can see similarities in DeLanda's theory as assemblages can just as easily refer to these micro level conversations, as they can to macro level organisational hierarchies and community structures (social systems). These assemblages or social systems entail more than just humans, but also artefacts from food to complex machinery or urban planning for instance.

Zizek [49] titles his analysis of Deleuze as 'Organs without bodies' in regard to the attention placed on the mechanics of these complex and dynamic assemblages. Moreover, Zizek invests in explaining the immaterial nature of the expressive dimension of the social world through illustrating content, meaning and signifiers (symbols). Zizek's immaterial approach largely ignores the material components. This is somewhat problematic in that interaction is reduced to a purely social level, without regard for the role that material artefacts have in conveying, facilitating and contributing to the social dimension. In this chapter, we argue that the material dimensions are equally as important as the immaterial – both of which are as expressive as each other. Material form and the actions produced through and in relation to this form are equally as cultural and socially expressive, as the linguistic constructs used to express them.

Here, it is important to return to the notion of territorialisation in order to understand that territorialisation refers to a stabilisation process of an assemblage [47]. This is where an assemblage reinforces its own identity at the same time as it ascertains identity within its components. There is a process and progress that can be seen in the stages of an assemblage and its territorialisation. For instance, a random meeting with an acquaintance on a street will start out lightly. It is framed by its context and environment – that of the urban area (spatial) and its timing (temporal) combined with other factors – and then takes on a stronger sense of territory (identity and narrative) through space, place and intensified dialogue. While both actors within the conversation may indeed hold different interpretations or understandings of the conversation in question, which in themselves manifest in differing experiences for each individual, a more standardised or routinised use of language and gestures begin to concretise. The discussion becomes a ceremony or synchronised performance, even if only for a short duration of time. Due to the ephemeral nature of assemblages and territorialisation in itself, the stabilisation that occurs within this interaction is an open one, free to morph, dissolve and re-territorialise when similar conditions and components come together once more. Yet, territorialisation in itself is always an active process [44].

This understanding of social interaction as occurring in actor networks (networks of human and non-human actors) and through assemblages formulations of various actors and components that in a sense, set the stage and frames of the interaction, are highly important when attempting to understand the aesthetic dimensions of interaction with social robots. This is due to the fact that one size does not fit all in terms of these aesthetic layers and how they are experienced, and indeed the interaction space when understanding it through assemblages. The material-expressive elements of the social robot design are one important element of the assemblage and its character. Yet, these material elements are continuously territorialised (stabilised and standardised), then deterritorialised (de-stabilised) depending on the configuration of components, changing of space and altering of time.

2.3.1 Embodiment within Assemblages

This understanding can be taken forward towards the cultural and philosophical scholarly fields of embodiment. In particular, Maurice Merleau-Ponty [15] in his phenomenology of perception describes how human lived experience exists in relationships between our body and the outside world. Thus, the body and its proximity to others (agents and objects) provides not simply the vehicle through which the world is perceived, but how it is perceived and made sense of in chains of material and immaterial relations. This close connection between the body and the outside world is termed, 'the intentional arc' [15]. The intentional arc explains the way that at all times the human body is undergoing constant and dynamic interactions with the world and its phenomena, and that humans learn the world not simply as mentally bound representations, but information that is stored throughout our entire body [50]. While seemingly dislocated from Weber's social action, in fact, it may be understood that the body, its expressions and relations are actually semantic organisms that *give meaning to action* [51, 52]. The body through this light also affects individual agency as both physical factors and limitations guide the way in which actors may affect and be affected by the world, allowing for interpretations of positive (affiliative) or negative (agonistic) interactions [20, 22] in accordance to the needs and affordances of the body [56, 57]. This may also be seen as inherent within the cognitive-affective theory of Appraisal in which all phenomena encountered in the surrounding world is appraised or evaluated either directly or indirectly through the primal concern of the body [35].

Another concept originated by Merleau-Ponty [15] that is useful for the discussion later on in this chapter is the body's tendency for maximal grip. This notion describes the way in which through the body, actors draw closer to situations via refining responses through practice. That is, when encountering phenomena over and over again, there is a tendency to learn through muscle and sensory memory and to optimise or refine our responses in a gestalt (or wholelike) way [50]. Once more, in light of the Appraisal Theory, this learned and refined way of being in relation to other bodied phenomena will also inform the cognitive-affective processes. These processes generate emotional responses and qualities within social encounters in relation to how the encounters or assemblages and their components connect with fulfilling or potentially damaging well-being. Interestingly, this is where embodiment and social interaction meet collective consciousness, as collective consciousness and its manifestation through collective enactments establishes the basis and purpose for the engagement with others to begin with.

Engaging with others through enactment that may be linguistic-based or non-linguistic-based enables a transaction of information that supplements and compliments the already known or existing information of an individual [53, 54]. On this note, we may look closer at the definition of social interaction and its components. Social interaction can be defined as an altering and dynamic series of meaning-making or semantic actions between two or more parties [55]. Interaction can be mediated by or transferred via technology (systems and artefacts). This is where we get back to the sociologists. Parsons' [23] conceptualisation of social interaction breaks the action down into unit acts. Unit acts define a selection process that engages in alternative means (varied choices) to a specified end (end-goal). Feeding into this process are the idea systems involved within the individual and within their collective consciousness (culture and social beliefs) and the situational conditions (circumstances in which the selection is being made). The level of engagement within this selection process hinges upon both the decision-making capabilities of the individual as well as the goal orientations – what is the desired outcome of interactional engagement?

In other words, the sociological perspectives put forward both by Parsons and developments to Parsons' model seen in Turner [11] understand that the material conditions and positioning of the body interact and intertwine with beliefs, values, norms and other symbol systems. Thus, through this embodied experiential and sociological lens, we may see that social interactions and their experience are constrained and framed through the material and immaterial conditions of bodies (organic and technological) and their connected symbolic systems (communication and representational expression). These in turn are affected by the changing circumstances of the bodies – changing biologies and evolving techno-cultural conditions [11]. In order to understand the aesthetic factors and dimensions of social robotics, it is vital to comprehend how the actors, their orientations and social actions (interactions) exist within these complex systems.

2.3.2 Embodied Interaction

The main trajectory of the efforts of this chapter is to argue for an approach to SoRAes that operates on embodied and discursive levels. In order to understand the aesthetic dimensions and components of social robot design, we *really* need to understand the essence and factors of social interaction in the first place. In order to derive the Social Robot Aesthetic Framework, we have mapped the core theoretical components in Figure 2.2. Through considering Shusterman's [56] notion of 'somaesthetics' (bodily aesthetics), and the understanding that the body is both a vessel for perception and bodily sensations, as well as an expressive vehicle that impacts the world around the body, we can model an understanding of embodied social interaction experience that is both affective and effective. The body is not merely a lump of flesh but an assemblage of material and immaterial properties (cultural, symbolic, values and systemic relationships) in its own right.

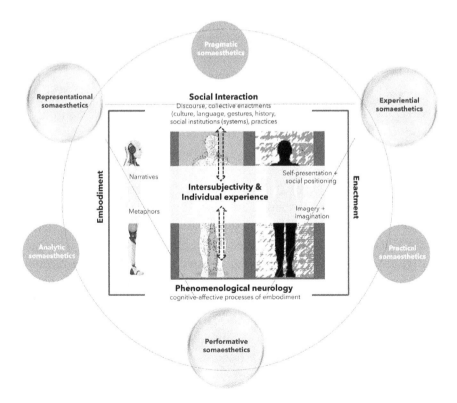

FIGURE 2.2   Embodiment, somaesthetics and social interaction. (Adapted from [53, 57].)

Immanuel Kant [58, 59] argued that the aesthetic was a type of knowledge. This was in contrast to earlier theories that posited the aesthetic as a particular ability within sensory perception [60]. The Aristotelian [61] view of the aesthetic was that of 'unity in manifold'. Resonating with the relatively modern theory of the 'mere exposure effect' [62], unity in manifold describes the way in which people recognise beauty in phenomena that they have been much exposed to. This corresponds with modern understandings that consider aesthetics in relation to cognitive-affective processes such as primary emotional reactions versus higher order cognitive emotions [35], as well as preference for the familiar [63]. These processes involve and concern the full body in relationship with the experienced phenomena of any interactional situation.

2.4 SOCIAL INTERACTION WITH COMPUTERS (AND ROBOTS) AND AESTHETICS

Interestingly, a bridge between robots, AI, aesthetics and art can be seen in recent developments that focus on robots in art creation. Whether the role of the robot is that of a 'brush tool' or as a powerful assistant, this creative level of conceptualising robotic capabilities is equally as fascinating as the development of AI itself. Vast speculation rests in the capacity for robotics and AI to take over the role of humans in creative processes (both from artists to designers). Yet, a firm argument for humans in fulfilling this role continues to exist within intentionality and consciousness – without intentionality, and intention, is any production creative? Subsequently, shifting this discussion into the context of the current chapter we may view the capacity for creativity, and or, the aesthetic experience generated from interaction with a perceived creative being (object, system) as a pivotal point for creating depth and cultural overall in social interactional design. Chen et al. [64] have identified four main ways of viewing robots in creative processes: (1) that of the programmed artist, or main producer of artistic output – still without own intentionality; (2) robots as co-creators – utilising AI and robotics to go beyond the limits of human cognition and bodily capacity; (3) robots as medium – the robots in themselves serving as the site for art; and (4) robots as human augmentation – creation and representation of the human ideal. Either way, this art-based robot insight provides fruit for thought in relation to the dynamics and discursive contribution robots may play within social interaction. For, aesthetic experience in itself is a creative process [13]. The more humans can see robots as co-creators, or even equal actors within assemblages, the more meaningful interactions with these objects (beings) become.

Moving back towards the building blocks of social interaction, over the years there have been many interesting discoveries relating to the nature of human intentionality and emotions in social interaction with technological objects. In fact from a research perspective, many scientists have discovered that often researchers can obtain more precise and consistent data about human-to-human interaction, when studying social interaction between humans and computers [65]. This is due to the technologically enabled possibilities of precise interactional (linguistic, expression, gesture) replication from one subject to the next. This means that the same conditions may be presented to human subjectivities repeatedly and indefinitely. Yet, while from the science lab perspective, computers, AI and subsequently robots, may offer advanced opportunities for gaining rich and robust research insight, in actuality and within the context of real life, these systems may fall short of offering a total and fulfilling social interactional experience. This is also so for the belief and utilisation of robots as so-called 'creative objects', or systems capable of creativity in themselves. As creativity is a highly complex and debated construct that both relies on conscious thought (intentionality, [66, 67]), and depending on the type of creativity in question (divergent versus convergent thinking, Big 'C' versus Little 'c', etc.) human knowledge retrieval, framing and indeed serendipity come into play.

However, endowing AI or robotics with the perceived capacity for creativity can be problematic from a social interaction point of view. In his 1976 paper titled, 'Artificial Intelligence Meets Natural Stupidity' Drew McDermott [68] coined the term 'wishful mnemonics' to explain the way that people not only have a tendency to believe that the machines are capable of more than they can, but through labelling the machines, their functions and data with human cognitive traits we are also misleading ourselves into believing that they are more human than they are. One of three mistakes McDermott accused AI researchers and developers of was labelling AI identifiers after concepts such as, 'understand', 'is a' (making a definite or concrete connection) or 'theorem'. What McDermott argued was that developers should name identifiers according to what the programs do, rather than what they would like them to do. In other words, back in the 1970s, as we still see today, there is a grandiose estimation of what people (particularly developers) feel computers, AI and robots should and are capable of doing. These do not match reality. They should therefore, not be used as they elevate peoples' expectations through wishful thinking. This results in disappointment as it establishes expectations for the interaction that are simply too high [5]. This is particularly the case for designing human-like android robots for social interaction, as a key goal within this process is to design a machine that is as close to human as possible.

Moreover, developing robotics that can imitate humans physically, and perhaps materially, is one matter, yet, establishing a social robotic system that is capable of not simply symbolically processing natural language, but understanding and interpreting it is another. To create real understanding and interpretation, there must be the capacity to attribute non-symbolic, immaterial and other associative properties and qualities. This would enable flexibility of thought, spontaneity in response and more than anything, creativity in social engagement. The bottom line in this argument that holds strong for this current article is that in order to fully understand and effectively develop the aesthetic properties of social robots, we need to move further than the formalistic material components, and indeed the mechanical capabilities, as particularly at this stage, we cannot place too much hope in the capacity of AI [69].

From a social aesthetic sense, the over-estimation of technological abilities and mistaking of database analytics as skills can be seen as a major drawback when designing these systems for social interaction. In fact, through a better understanding of humans and adjustment of the expressive communication around social robotic systems (i.e. the language and labels that describe these systems to people), a richer, more fulfilling experience can be established through deflating estimations in order to lower expectations. Moreover, it is often forgotten that some of the characteristics that contribute to fulfilment, satisfaction and positive experience in social interactions are actually the randomness and unpredictability of human imperfection [70, 71].

To really understand this from the perspective of aesthetics, we must first define what we mean by aesthetics. Aesthetics in itself is a broad field of philosophical study that is often connected with artwork and notions of beauty. Yet, there are many more understandings that incorporate anything from the qualities of experience, judgement and values to object-based understandings, expressions of culture and taste [72]. Here, the term 'aesthetics' links to notions of immediacy in experience. This immediacy has been described by Davide Panagia [73] as:

> ... the temporality of an aesthetics of politics. When an appearance advenes, it strikes an impression on a sensorial apparatus, variously conceived. In doing so, it disarticulates our senses of

constancy, continuity, and commonality. The immediacy of an aesthetics of politics is thus rooted in an ontology of discontinuity.

In HCI terminology, we may easily refer to research on presence and immersion through the 'experience of being there' [74]. This is an all engaging experience in which artificially constructed or not, the interaction and events themselves become merged with our embodied realities. Philosopher David Hume [75] described the concept of *taste* (as in preference) as a form of internal sense. If, on a simplistic level, we understand that there are five external (direct) senses – sight, taste (tongue-based), olfactory, touch, sound – then an 'internal' sense relies on mentally stored information (i.e. knowledge and associations from previous experiences, and other representational contents such as sense data [76, 77] in order to function). That is, an aesthetic experience combines sensory information from the external and internal (reflex or secondary) senses to form an embodied impression, sensations and meaning within encounters. Thomas Reid [78] argued that:

> Beauty or deformity in an object, results from its nature or structure. To perceive the beauty therefore, we must perceive the nature or structure from which it results. In this the internal sense differs from the external. Our external senses may discover qualities which do not depend upon any antecedent perception …. But it is impossible to perceive the beauty of an object, without perceiving the object, or at least conceiving it.

It is precisely this point in the nature of aesthetics that rely on the human perceiver and experiencer that we emphasise in this chapter. For, in a certain moment at a given time, more people within a study sample may respond positively to a certain social robot design than others. Yet, at another moment, and potentially with another group of people these preferences, and tastes, may have changed. For this reason it is important to understand the combination of sensory information and mentally bound antecedents to establish a formula, or framework, that describes how humans experience the aesthetics of social robot design.

In reflection of these aesthetic discussions, beauty itself is a highly complex construct, both in terms of its understanding, as well as in terms of the way it presents itself through artefacts, systems, beings and other phenomena. While the ability to perceive and/or conceive the nature and structure of artefacts presents one part of aesthetic engagement, it does not explain beauty and the experience of beauty fully in itself. This is due to the fact that the combination of internal and external senses in aesthetic experience is highly dynamic, contextually, socially and psychologically dependent and the qualities (qualia) of these experiences are in turn, pertinently subjective. Aesthetics emerged through discourse over 200 years ago along with major societal shifts regarding the institutionalisation of art [79]. These discussions were used as a vehicle through which to intellectualise creative expression, distinguish between artistic or intentionally creative efforts and other domains (e.g. handicraft and mechanical manual labour), and to create distinctions on cultural and societal levels – coupling sophistication of creative expression with discussions on *taste* and the ability to appreciate the structures and mechanics of these pieces (higher order cognition and emotions).

2.4.1 Structuring Interaction and Discursive Aesthetics

Engagement with robots, and even AI when looking at the role of the body in enabling the human mind and cognitive function, is a fully embodied process. This includes engagement in interaction. Returning back to McDermott [68] we can see that from the perspective of human experience, and indeed, the experience of socially interacting with other humans, there is a fine line between intellectual sophistication and stimulation, and imperfection within human discourse. Prominent characteristics of AI and traditional computational technology hold in their symmetry and accuracy of calculation and semantic analysis. Whereas, human beings are prone to asymmetry (both physically and cognitively as seen in biases for instance). These are often perceived in terms of quirkiness or often referred to 'common sense' [69]. Interestingly, in Nass and Yen's [1] sociological research on human-to-human interaction, their team discovered that the perfect confederate to study was a computer. This is due to the fact that computers do not alter. Rather, computers remain consistent in content, state and demographic characteristics. Computers are valuable from the social interaction perspective as they can evoke diverse social reactions and responses that may be repeated in exactly the same action continuously (24/7). Furthermore, computers are not affected by their subconscious responses, and have the capacity to avoid unconscious biases presented by users (humans). Finally, no matter what the communicational output is, computers operate via rules. From a programming perspective, there is no ambiguity within the machine's logic, and while humans and humans as users may not be able to see this logic, transparency through knowledge of the stability of machine behaviour should create an underlying sense of safety through consistency. For, as Nass [65] stated, 'Rules are incredibly powerful!'

Computers can however be programmed to give 'asymmetric' or quirky questions and responses, making their interaction seem realistic, as has been discovered in relation to the Turing Test, whereby human errors and oddities have been incorporated in the computer responses to give its communication an air of human authenticity [80, 81]. If we think of interaction from the perspective of learning, and the potential of learning something new occurring through abnormalities in discussion such as mistakes, new details to older stories, misunderstandings, poor grammar, etc. then it can be assumed that aesthetically, these imperfections have multiple aesthetic qualities. These qualities range from this excitement of anticipation of discovering more (see e.g. [63]), stimulating higher order cognitive-affective processes similar to those associative processes that occur during art appreciation. There are also primary emotional reactions (or close to primary) by the human recognising the AI as imperfect, thus, not posing a threat to the human's existence. To break this down into the main points of connection between human cognition and aesthetic experience, we can see that some of the key components of human understanding contributing to interactional and aesthetic experience are [65]:

- Intuitive physics, biology and psychology
- Mental models of cause and effect
- Vast world-knowledge
- Abstraction and analogy

These main points can be seen throughout this chapter's descriptions on social interaction and aesthetics to varying degrees. Yet, to understand how they operate in the context of SoRAes, we can look closer at preferences and human emotional responses to certain types of interactions, and interactional structures. To illustrate this, Nass highlighted the underlying structures and rules for what we may understand as the *aesthetic qualities of interaction*. These rules are as follows:

- Humans evaluate machine intelligence as intelligence (similar to 'Artificial intelligence versus natural stupidity') regardless of whether or not they feel it is authentic, sincere or random.

- There is something smart about negativity – cruel equals brilliance and when the computer blames the human, the computer is the genius.

- People are willing to pay more for computers that praise them.

- Negativity stays in the brain[2] – when people are criticised their memory of the event(s) increase.

- People's emotions and emotional disposition should be matched – e.g. happy people like happy people (machines) and vice versa.

These types of scientific findings should be drawn upon when designing social robots for desirable aesthetic social interactional experiences. Human science-based traditions and theories such as Social Cognition Theory that argue that people see reflections of the self in others, should be carefully considered. This additionally leads to more concrete and practical questions such as, what words, register and approach should be used when designing robot communication? And, indeed, should social robots look like and mimic people, or should they have an identity of their own? Interestingly, the matter of human tendency to see themselves in others and objects, and moreover to be attracted to this *self* in others has been discussed in terms of the *self as an aesthetic effect* [84]. There is a human need for self-validation, which is one of the drives for embodied social interaction [85].

2.5 SOCIAL ROBOT AESTHETIC FRAMEWORK (SoRAes)

As seen so far in this chapter, literature and theory in the fields of social interaction, embodiment and aesthetics are rich and varied. While in fact, more of this classical literature should be brought into contemporary discussion, particularly when considering the vital role of the human mind in the development of emerging intelligent technologies, there should be a way of synthesising it in order to achieve practical outcomes. For this very practical reason, we see it necessary to break down the human social and embodied components of interaction with robots into biteable chunks that may form a scaffolding for making more precise design decisions in social robot development. In fact, we have developed the Social Robot Aesthetic Framework (SoRAes – pronounced, 'So Raise', see Figure 2.3) in order to isolate the factors contributing to the complex, multilayered and varied understanding of aesthetic experience in social robot interaction that accounts for more than just 'skin deep' design elements.

In this framework we chart the dimensions related to intersubjective interaction in human–robot interaction. The created framework derives

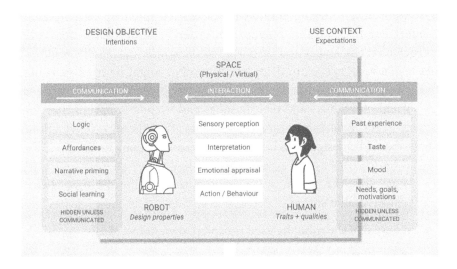

FIGURE 2.3   Social Robot Aesthetic (SoRAes) Framework.

from previous works in product and interaction design, aesthetics and social psychology. The purpose of the framework is to map the aesthetic and interactional properties we need to take in account when designing social robots. In this sub-chapter we explain the significance of each dimension, using examples to clarify what the different aspects might mean and how to use them in practice.

SoRAes represents assemblages of human–robot social interaction from a somaesthetic perspective. The main components of the SoRAes Framework are: use context – expectations (intention and motivation of use); design objectives – intentions (design intentions); space – physical/virtual; robot design properties; human traits and qualities; and the sensory aesthetic dimensions. The following sections describe these components. This is achieved through providing examples specific to the current COVID-19 pandemic in order to highlight the potential of the framework for designing more effective and affective social interaction with robots for these challenging circumstances. Guiding this framework in practice is an ontology realised through sets of questions that correspond with each component of the framework. These are presented in conjunction with the descriptions below.

2.5.1 Use Context – Expectations (Use Intention and Motivation)

We need to start from charting the user needs. For example, given the current pandemic, we want to ease the loneliness of elderly people and others living alone who cannot leave their home or have visitors during the lockdown. The main design goal is to create a robot that can be used by people who might have differing abilities (deteriorating mobility, hearing and/or sight), cognitive decline (memory disorders) and/or even people with interpersonal challenges and inabilities to recognise social and emotional cues (e.g. autism spectrum disorder). The robot might be used as a substitute for other human companions, or it may indeed be a link between the isolated individuals and their families and friends. A part of charting the user needs involves posing questions that affect the ways in which the robots should be designed in light of use. These questions include:

- What does the user want to accomplish by using the robot (what problem will it solve)?

- Where will the robot be used (hospital, own home, etc.)?

- Will other people be using the same robot? Is it public (hospitals, schools), private (own home, private events) or shared (private but can be used by several people, e.g. family members)?

- Should the robot be specialised in one task only, or be able to cater to multiple needs (e.g. companion + physical assistance)?

These are just a few questions among many that may be posed to decipher the physical and contextual boundaries of the embodied social interactional experience expected to be encountered during use.

2.5.2 Design Objective – Intentions (Designer Expectations of Use and User Experience)

The design objective or design (designer) intention is one of the most common discussed factors in cognitive science. Design intention has been researched from the perspectives of communication in design and user experience (see e.g. [86]) to intentionality in AI (see e.g. [87]). To establish a practical basis for the design objective we need to ask the following questions:

- What are we trying to accomplish – what problem needs to be solved? (in the COVID-19 case, very likely loneliness induced by social distancing).

- Are we intending to develop a commercial or non-profit product? → who is the customer and who is the end user (revenue model)?

- What is the minimum viable product that we can aspire towards? → the simplest solution to build that solves one part of the problem?

- What is the design and development budget/resources/funding? →
  what can be achieved with the resources available?

After we know what we are designing to whom, why and what the available
resources are, we can proceed to analyse factors that can affect (positively
or negatively) the desired result. This also sets up the scene for understanding the assemblage at hand, affording certain types of understandings of
the factors involved in the social interactions. This aids in ascertaining
insight into the *framing* of both the social interaction itself as well as some
levels of the conscious experience occurring within the human user. For,
the more information we have about the humans engaged in these interactions, the more we can know what, how and why the person experiences
the interaction in the way that they do.

2.5.2.1 Space (Physical/Virtual)

Interaction happens always in space and place, be it fully physical or partly
virtual. Partly virtual is referred to here, due to the user's body always
being in some physical space, of which properties have an effect on the
success and effects of communication and interaction. If the communication takes place partly virtually (e.g. through VR glasses), we need to take
into account the properties of both the physical and virtual space. For this,
designers and developers should answer the following questions:

- Where does the interaction take place?
  - Physical: own home, office, hospital, open air, one room or sev-
    eral, one kind of environment or in several different ones
- Is this virtual? → what kind of virtual space/environment?
- What kinds of objects and phenomena can be perceived in the use
  environment? Artefacts, other people, spacious or crowded, temper-
  ature, quiet or noisy, etc.
- How/where does the user get into the space? Travel time, check in,
  opening computer/software, logging in, etc.
- How does the robot relate to the space? Does it move or stay in one
  place? Does it need to interact with/react to other objects in the space?

When we are talking about human–robot interaction, the dimensions that
affect reaching the desired result can be divided into three parts. On the

right-hand side we have the robot agent, with its built-in properties. On the left-hand side we have the human agent, with their personal traits and accumulated experiences. These remain unknown to the other agent until they are being communicated in some way, whether we are aware of the information exchanged or not. Pictured in the middle of the framework is the interaction, or exchange of information, which takes place between the agents. The interaction in the middle means all information that is received via perceiving the other agent in some way, conscious or unconscious for the human and via perceptual (sound, visual, even possibly temperature and vibration, etc.) sensors and processors for the robot. The process can be modelled in roughly the same way for each human interactor on the levels of sensory perception, symbolic processing and behaviour. First, sensory input is received, then the received data is interpreted (attached to semantic meaning and alternate options for behavioural response), which in turn is coupled with emotional-aesthetic reaction within the human. Finally, we make an assessment of the situation using the emotional reaction as a cue, and act accordingly.

For the human agent, sensory data is received multi-modally, and the emotional reaction is formed either immediately or through associative processes depending on the type of encounter, design and actions. This is as the result of the automatic interpretation of this complicated, intricate data, unconsciously performed by our brain. Depending on the person's level of self-awareness (refer to symbolic interactionism, i.e. [26]), it is possible to make conscious effort to intercept this process before acting on the impulse roused by the initial emotional reaction (primary response triggering basic emotions) and use logical thinking to come up with other possible interpretations (associative higher order thinking seen in traditional aesthetics).

For the robotic agent, the data is collected via electronic sensors. The kind of data that is possible to collect is dependent on the technical properties of the robot. After collecting data, the robot needs to be able to make a real time interpretation of what the data means in the context of this particular interaction. Instead of the emotional appraisal happening automatically in the human counterpart, the robot needs to make an assessment of what kind of actions it needs to perform in order to appropriately react to the state of the human agent. This is what we call *social-emotional awareness* within the SoRAes design. This links to the social learning component that will soon be discussed.

Interpretation and the appraisal process that leads to the actions that form the communication between the agents, happens by sensorily perceiving physical attributes and connecting these attributes to meanings and alternative action possibilities. Here, we come to the importance of aesthetics, as aesthetic experience can be seen as having a positive emotional reaction to the things perceived in our environment which our brain interprets as beneficial to our survival or well-being (e.g. [35]). When designing robots, we should consider how we can best communicate the functionality of the robot to the user, to make the user experience as intuitive and pleasant as possible. The best design can be intuitively understood in much the same way as social situations that feel predictable and familiar to us. These types of interactions are perceived as the most pleasant [63].

2.5.3 Robot Design Properties

We have divided the robot design properties into several components that contribute to aesthetic experience in interaction. These are logic, affordances, narrative priming and social learning. Their associated ontological questions are as follows:

- Logic
  - How does robot 'intelligence' work?
  - How does the design and functionalities operate in relation to human thought?
  - What are the patterns, traits and protocol of the robot's operations?
- Affordances
  - How is the robot constructed?
  - What kind of tasks is it able to perform?
  - What does it *give* the human user, and *enable* them to do?
- Narrative priming
  - Do we give the user some background information on the robot, like details of its personality and its origins (cultural, make-believe, history of form)?
  - Does the user know something about the designer or company who made the robot?
  - Can brand identity play a role in social robotics?

- Social learning

  - Does the robot remember the users or their preferences if they have met before?

  - Can the robot form preconceptions? (e.g. after meeting three girls who like playing with dolls, does it suggest playing with dolls to the fourth girl also?)

  - What types of words and language can the robot pick up to assimilate communication with the human?

Thus, the logic is about understanding the cognitive logic or rules of information flow, understanding, processing and behaviour of the social robot design from both holistic and material cultural expressive perspectives [11, 23]. By holistic we mean, the overall behaviour – movement, speech, language, gestures, etc. In terms of material cultural expressive perspectives we refer to the particular details of the robot's form and design, i.e. materials, shapes, psychological principles of form (e.g. symmetry and facial features, appealing to paedomorphosis [baby face bias] and Kawaii [Japanese cute], etc.).

Affordances derives both through James Gibson's [88] Ecological Theory, as well as Donald Norman's [89, 90] discussions on the role of affordances in design, in which humans perceive phenomena in terms of what they afford, or offer them. This may be in terms of use value or social-expressive value. As Gibson stresses, we identify phenomena based on what we can do with it, and subsequently what it does for us. Thereby, a chair is perceived and interpreted often primarily in terms of whether or not we can sit on it. Immaterial qualities, values and affordances implicated in the chair's design may be seen in anything from the material used to create the chair, trademark form (e.g. the iconic Eames chair, or the James Bond-like Eero Aarnio fabric bubble chair), or even novelty in the functionality and use of the chair. Similarly, social robots – their form, and even capabilities of cognition, emotion and discussion – will be interpreted in terms of what they afford the human user. Particularly in the COVID-19 pandemic period and from a social perspective, the robot may be seen as fulfilling (affording) social needs in terms of providing companionship through meaningful discussion and/or affording the possibility for individuals to express their feelings about the situation. From this social aesthetic perspective, we may understand that oftentimes social fulfilment comes through the ability to reveal our inner selves and talk through our problems without judgement[3]. For this reason, psychologists are increasingly in demand.

Narrative priming in itself constantly occurs through people's exposure to media and social interaction with other humans. We are continuously primed through stories and anecdotes on the nature of robots. Yet, narrative priming may also be used strategically to shape the way in which people attach meaning to and make sense of the social robots at hand. If looking at the doll industry for instance, the iconic Cabbage Patch kids were sold with a birth certificate that established date of birth and name. Looking back further in history, little Russian nesting dolls (Matryoshka) with their many layers provided multidimensional and multi-character build up to the identity and experience of the dolls. Narrative is also a strong aesthetic factor in human–robot fields such as sex robots in which humans form deeper relationships with the robots based on either a previously established narrative, or the narrative the individual themselves create in interaction with the robot (see, e.g. [92]). During times of the COVID-19 and the inability to escape the physical living conditions of one's home, the possibility to escape through narrative and imagination is all the more appealing.

2.5.4 Human Traits and Qualities

2.5.4.1 Past Experiences

The past experiences of a person highly affect the way one interprets sensory information involved in encounters with various phenomena. Our aesthetic preferences are influenced by the kinds of environments we have been in when experiencing strong positive or negative emotions. The elderly person in our example might find the earthly colours and scents from their childhood farmhouse as safe and pleasant. Yet, the presence of shiny surfaces and bright lighting may be associated with unpleasant hospital visits. An urban youth might associate these same attributes of earthly smells and agricultural buildings as old-fashioned, unrefined or unclean versus modern, reliable and high-class. Likewise, the ways in which an individual approaches a social robot and then engages in longitudinal interactions with the robot also relies heavily at first on these previous experiences. Biases and prejudices against the technology held from prior experience (either first-hand or second-hand through news and social discussion) may be overwritten with continued exposure, use and also the conditions. Social isolation causes anxiety [11] for which people may be actively seeking solutions, making them more willing to engage in social robot interaction despite prior opinions.

2.5.4.2 Culture

The cultural background of the individual affects the way that they interpret different social and visual cues, for example body language, colour preferences, even the amount of perfume someone wears. This is due to the fact that many of our readings of material and behaviour, in addition to the way that we behave ourselves, are based on social conventions, routines, rituals and consensus [93]. This too, informs the 'framing' of the social interactional assemblage at hand. Perception and experience of materials, shapes (e.g. facial form and ethnically or culturally specific features etc.) and colours is not simply about preference, but the ways in which we as humans are culturally programmed to attribute meaning to these specific forms. This occurs through the rituals, behaviour and beliefs that are mentioned above [94, 95]. This is in addition to having a firmer evolutionary psychological basis that both consciously and subconsciously tells an individual as to whether or not they are encountering friend, family, foe or even a potential mate [96]. Likewise, depending on context, readings of the materials, forms and their values may drastically change. Furthermore, in terms of the current COVID-19 social robot discussion, it needs to be acknowledged that some cultures are more prepared for the eventuality of robots fulfilling human social needs than others. For instance, we can see this in Chinese and Japanese cultures to name two, where there are already long traditions in engaging in robot interaction for social purposes [97, 98].

2.5.4.3 Taste (Preferences)

Taste is one of the main aspects of classical discussions on aesthetics [72]. On a basic and practical level, taste is formed or cultivated in the context of the person's surrounding cultural and social environments. Taste has been discussed equally as much in relation to art [75] as it has in relation to social class [99]. While past experiences contribute to the underlying emotional landscape from which our aesthetic emotions spring, our social environment dictates the boundaries of desirable and acceptable phenomena as well as its expression, and how we may (should) react to these. These social environments additionally regulate the types of emotions that are considered acceptable to reveal or show to others around us. The youth from the previous example might associate a bold flower pattern with his grandmother's musty old-fashioned curtains but start finding it fresh and exciting after seeing similar patterns worn by their favourite social media influencer. Thus, we already see the overlaps and interrelations between cultural levels such as narrative priming, culture itself and the factors that contribute to taste formation.

2.5.4.4 Mood

Our perceptions are affected by our current internal state. If someone had a stressful and challenging day of work behind them, they might long for a quiet relaxing evening at home. But at times when their life feels dull and uneventful, they navigate towards more exciting and stimulating experiences. The concept of mood is constantly confused with that of emotion [100]. Yet, one way of explaining the difference is through the great semiotician, Charles Sanders Peirce's [101] explanation of shades of colour. Peirce described moods at states of mind that are similar to colours, for instance the shade of blue. For instance, if someone wakes up in the morning experiencing the shade of blue – perhaps from a dream, or perhaps from occurrences of the day before – this shade will taint the perception of the phenomena and events to follow within the day. This influences the ways in which we emotionally experience our encounters with phenomena.

2.5.4.5 Needs, Goals, and Motivations

People always have a reason for engaging with technology, and particularly for using a robot. This affects the way the suitability of the robot is evaluated. People vary greatly in their expectations towards robots. Whether they want to use one as a social companion or a teaching assistant, there are dynamic and altering sets of criteria that humans anticipate within the design and interaction circumstances. This hinges upon the match of what the robot and its design affords in regards to needs, goals and motivations of the individual. The evaluation of the appropriateness to needs, goals and motivations ties in with Appraisal and the perceiving of affordances. Someone may need conversation to feel closeness to others. Others might want to play games or do some other activities to achieve that same feeling. For others owning a certain kind of robot might signal social or financial status or personal taste. In reflection of an example given earlier, a social robot may fulfil the purpose of enabling the human user to feel heard during the times of the pandemic crisis. Another engaging in more intimate actions with robots may be fulfilling the need to feel wanted, and to belong. Thus, a form of responsiveness within the robot's design, or responsiveness within the design and development team to truly understand the target groups for whom they are developing is crucial.

2.5.5 Aesthetic Dimension (and Multisensory Experience)

When discussing aesthetic dimensions we refer to the multisensory experiences in interaction situations that can have either positive or negative effects on the outcomes exchange. These are the dimensions that one should consider when designing social robots and, additionally, the spaces and environments in which they are used. Thus, we should not think of the aesthetics of social robot design in a vacuum, rather than from the *assemblage* perspective in which environment, context, people and other objects are all equal actors in forming the interactional experience.

Not only do people attribute meaning to the robot designs, but materials, forms and linguistic expressions of the machines operate in relation to and against the formal properties of the surroundings. For instance, while being cute, a large fluffy teddy bear robot may be off putting within the context of intensive care. The smell of heated electrics and warm plastic generated by the robot body may not be appetising in a restaurant setting etc. In order to address this we list the basic five external senses – sight, sound, touch, smell and taste – and the types of information that may be collected through them. In relation to these we outline the types of emotional responses that multisensory inputs can evoke in the person perceiving them. Finally, we take a look at the meaning and significance of multimodality in the human-social robot interaction process, and how the sensory experience is perceived across the different modalities.

2.5.5.1 Sight

The sense of sight is often considered the dominant human sense, and earlier research has proven so in many contexts (see e.g. [102–104]). This is what is referred to as sensory dominance [105]. Sight enables the ability to gain a total picture, or collection of various parts and wholes with one glance. In fact, as most sighted individuals have experienced (e.g. in virtual reality interactions), when engaged in the act of viewing, it is easy to become consciously immersed in the visual sensory information. Other sensory input may remain on the levels of either subconscious or unconscious experience. Visual sensory design factors that should be considered from the human perspective include:

- colour psychology of spaces and objects
- visually perceived materials
- social cues of colours

- spatial perception (is the space crowded or roomy)
- social distance (cultural differences)
- body language, mirroring
- time lag
- uncanny valley

This visual information prepares the human and their body for particular types of behaviour when engaging in social robot interaction. In turn, as in the theory of somaesthetics, this preparation, behaviour and expression of the body shapes the way in which the interaction is experienced [57].

2.5.5.2 Hearing

Sound also plays a major role in human perception, and often goes relatively unnoticed in encounters and situations that are focused on or framed by the visual sense [105]. Think of the way in which music is used as a narrative experiential device in film and theatre. Beyond the subconscious role of sound as a sensory enhancer, sound also plays an important interactional role in human communication. Audio factors that should be carefully accounted for in the robot design include:

- speaking voice: tone and colour, gender, age, accent, language, volume
- mechanical sounds from the robot body
- use of other sounds: music, nature sounds, alarms and signals
- use environment soundscape (background noises): quiet or loud, echoing, can you hear chatter, traffic, etc.

These all play crucial roles in the experience of the social robotic experience assemblage, and may mean the difference between for instance trust, or lack thereof, in the object based on the gender and age of the voice. Mechanical sounds may be off-putting or even eerie, contributing to a heightened sense of the uncanny when combined with human-like visuals.

2.5.5.3 Touch

Touch is one of the integral senses in terms of relationship forming. Through touch, for instance, handshakes, taps on the shoulder or even hugs, the hormone called oxytocin is released [106]. This is a hormone that plays a role in childbirth as well as breastfeeding. It induces a sense of bond between the two individuals engaged in touch and additionally creates a sense of emotional bond between humans and objects [107]. Touch is known as the sense that pre-determines purchase of goods [108]. Gentle touch is also associated with decreasing stress [109]. There are also cross-modal correspondences [110] – interactions between the senses – that induce experiences of perceived touch, or perceived visual information through touch, which are interesting to observe in material design. Some aesthetic factors to consider in relation to touch are:

- visual perception of a material can produce a physical sensation
- temperature has an impact on emotions
- psychology, and the psycho-physiology of touch
- social touch: aggression, pressure, safety, etc.

While touch is traditionally categorised as one sense within the basic external five sense understanding of the senses, indeed, in more sophisticated sensory models, the tactile sense comprises several composites (or senses). There is the vestibular sense, or sense of balance and movement [111], and the sense of temperature (thermoception, [112]) to name some.

2.5.5.4 Smell

Smell is a chemical sense – one that relies on sensory receptors that react with molecules in the substances humans inhale [113]. Smell plays a highly important yet greatly overlooked role in emotional experience, and particularly interaction with others, due to the fact that olfactory information is processed in an area of the brain that rests closest to the limbic system [114]. The limbic system is the area of the brain that processes emotional information, making associations between input and attributed emotional experience. What is more, the sense of smell is the most direct channel between the outside world and the limbic system. Given the cognitive role of emotions in for instance, attention, memory and recall, this means that smell, which is closely connected to emotion in the brain (emotional associations taking place through smell), also heightens recall and cognitive associations [115]. Many may have experienced times in which the smell of a particular perfume may take us back to a particular childhood memory of our mother and the emotions attached to this memory [116]. Smells can usually only be perceived when people are in closer contact with the per-ceived phenomena. Olfactory factors that should be considered from the SoRAes perspective are:

- materials – plastic, metal, wood, perfume, human-like?

- possibilities with aromatherapy, etc.

- use environment: fresh or stuffy air (ventilation)

- psychology of smell (bakery, new car smell, etc.)

2.5.5.5 Taste

There is an old saying, 'The way to a man's heart is through his stomach'. The sense of taste is the most intimate sense when related to social interaction [117]. It may usually only be reserved for very intimate situ-ations on the one hand, or can be seen as a social connector, i.e. through the cultural practice of food (cooking and joint dining) on the other [118]. However, because of the multimodality of senses, we can evoke the sen-sations associated with different tastes also through visual and olfactory cues. In fact, taste and flavour are two concepts regularly mistaken for one another. Yet, flavour in contrast to taste, is the combination of taste and smell [119]. Additionally, connections to emotions and personalities have also been made to taste [120]. Think about, for example, how a per-son or an emotion could be sweet, bitter or sour. The assemblage of social interactions may boost in memorability and meaning if taste is combined with smell to produce flavour in interaction, perhaps through thinking of robots in context – restaurants, parties, home chefs – or even as flavoured love companion (sex) robots.

2.6 DISCUSSION

Aesthetic considerations involved in designing robots for social interac-tion with humans is expansive and complex on many levels, from the human psycho-biological make up itself, to social levels, technological and contextual levels. If considering an underlying design objective for the development of social robots as being that of improving the social wellbe-ing of humans, aesthetic experience and its relationship to emotions is one of the main starting points for concretely endeavouring this feat. Through using our knowledge of emotional responses created by design choices, we can create different kinds of user experiences that can have various positive impacts on an individual's mental state and overall physiological well-being. This is achieved through the impact of social interaction, sense of belongingness and intellectual engagement in conversation as well as that of situated multisensory experience on the body. Through the current knowledge presented in this article we can also prevent making mistakes in the robot design that might accidentally work against the desired effect.

The purpose of this chapter was to merge insight from sociological, philosophical, cognitive scientific and cultural studies traditions to explain the aesthetic dimensions of social interaction between humans and robots. In this particular chapter, the emphasis is on understanding these dimensions in the context of the COVID-19 pandemic crisis. This chapter has linked traditions of human thought and theory to the practical development of a framework for aesthetic design in social robot interaction. The goal of this chapter was to go beyond prominent research into surface level design issues such as external form and even voice, to concentrate on the logical and semantic dimensions of social interaction. The framework we present here, SoRAes, aids in designing for social interactional and aesthetic framing. SoRAes incorporates factors of linguistics, culture, social components (ANT – the assemblage of given situations in which all actors/factors equally influence the composition) and, indeed, embodied multisensory experience itself.

In an academic setting as in the practical field of technological development, it may be understandable to gravitate towards seemingly simpler solutions that are easier to control when there is a need for measurable results. However, overlooking the vague and shifting nature of design and aesthetic experience, we might inadvertently close our eyes to the more serious issues that, when taken into consideration, might compromise the relevance and accuracy of the achieved results and inferences. When researching the human reactions to social robots, especially when it comes to the negative effects and associations that keep coming up over and over again like in the case of uncanny valley, to be able to correct the problem we must first have a complete understanding of what the problem actually is. That will only be possible after having some kind of comprehension about all the possible variables that might affect the outcome (human experience) in the real world usage and research situations. The SoRAes framework is an attempt to map these dimensions in a way that would make it easier for engineers, designers and researchers to plan and design human–robot interaction scenarios and make aesthetic decisions that effectively work towards achieving the intended goal.

In this chapter, we gave a brief introduction to the different modalities related to the aesthetic experience and the complex sociological, psychological and philosophical theories surrounding them. There is a plethora of research available considering the psychology of modalities, like colour and material psychology, but connecting and understanding the vast multimodal elements in the context relevant to social robot design remains largely unexplored. One worthy direction to approach the exploration of the design process further, could be the utilisation of character design and narrative techniques combined with product design principles. When designing and building a robot with affective qualities, we are in fact creating a fictitious character, using aesthetic means to evoke feelings in the user. From another practical perspective this means that we should not shy from using the expertise of artists, writers and directors to guide us in making the most important design decisions. For designing social interactional aesthetic experience with robots, is like creating a meaningful, engaging and emotional chapter of life.

ACKNOWLEDGEMENTS

The authors would like to thank the Professor Pekka Abrahamsson and the AI Ethics at the University of Jyväskylä for supporting the work in this article.

NOTES

1. We may even think beyond human actors, as in Action Network Theory (ANT), whereby everything – both human and non-human (e.g., technological) can be considered an equal actor, or equally influential within their respective ecosystem. See for instance, [24, 25].
2. This was observed by Rousi [82] in relation to elevator travel, where negative phenomena and events trigger primal cognitive-affective responses such as fear, disgust and anxiety, that in turn release adrenaline charging humans [83] to respond (freeze, flight, fight), strengthening us, sharpening attention and activating information storage that leads to long-term memory recall [84].
3. Think of verbal catharsis and the role of the psychologist as a listener and mirror for psychological (and social) cleansing [91].

REFERENCES

1. Nass, C., and Yen, C., 2010, The man who lied to his laptop: What we can learn about ourselves from our machines (London: Penguin).
2. Stern, D., 2005, Intersubjectivity. In The American psychiatric publishing textbook of psychoanalysis (Washington, DC: American Psychiatric Publishing, Inc., 77–92).

3. Schiffrin, D., 1990, The principle of intersubjectivity in communication and conversation. Semiotica, 80(1/2), 121–151.

4. Zahavi, D., 2001, Beyond empathy. Phenomenological approaches to inter-subjectivity. Journal of Consciousness Studies, 8(5–6), 151–167.

5. Pearson, J., Hu, J., Branigan, H. P., Pickering, M. J., and Nass, C. I., 2006, Adaptive language behavior in HCI: how expectations and beliefs about a system affect users' word choice. In Proceedings of the SIGCHI Conference on Human Factors in Computing Systems (ACM, 1177–1180).

6. Delia, J. G., Clark, R. A., and Switzer, D. E., 1974, Cognitive complexity and impression formation in informal social interaction. Communications Monographs, 41(4), 299–308.

7. Tractinsky, N., 2004, Toward the study of aesthetics in information technology. In ICIS Proceedings, 62.

8. Birkin, G., 2010, Aesthetic complexity: Practice and perception in art & design (Nottingham Trent: Nottingham Trent University).

9. Nørskov, M., 2017, Social robots: Boundaries, potential, challenges (Milton Park: Taylor & Francis).

10. Ray, C., Mondada, F., and Siegwart, R., 2008, What do people expect from robots?. In 2008 IEEE/RSJ International Conference on Intelligent Robots and Systems (IEEE, 3816–3821).

11. Turner, J. H., 1988, A theory of social interaction (Redwood City, CA: Stanford University Press).

12. Sailer, K., 2011, Creativity as social and spatial process. Facilities, 29(1–2), 6–18.

13. Dewey, J., and Martin, D., 1934, Art as experience (Vol. 10). (New York, NY: Minton, Balch, 1925–1953).

14. Merleau-Ponty, M., 1964, Signs. Transl. Ed. R.C. McCleary. Evanston, IL: Northwestern University Press.

15. Merleau-Ponty, M., 2012, The Phenomenology of Perception, Translated and Edited by D.A. Landes (London: Routledge).

16. Döring, N., 2020, How is the COVID-19 pandemic affecting our sexualities? An overview of the current media narratives and research hypotheses. Archives of Sexual Behavior, 49(8), 2765–2778.

17. Venkatesh, A., and Edirappuli, S., 2020, Social distancing in covid-19: what are the mental health implications? BMJ, 369, 1. DOI: 10.1136/bmj.m1379

18. Alenljung, B., Lindblom, J., Andreasson, R., and Ziemke, T., 2019, User experience in social human-robot interaction. In Rapid automation: Concepts, methodologies, tools, and applications (Hershey, PN: IGI Global, 1468–1490).

19. Habermas, J., 1979, Communication and the evolution of society (Vol. 572). (Boston, MA: Beacon Press).

20. Wey, T. W., Jordán, F., and Blumstein, D. T., 2019, Transitivity and structural balance in marmot social networks. Behavioral Ecology and Sociobiology, 73(6), 1–13.

21. Weber, M., 1991, Zur Neuordnung Deutschlands: Schriften und Reden 1918-1920 (Vol. 16). (Tübingen: Mohr Siebeck).

22. Weber, M., 1978, Economy and society: An outline of interpretive sociology (Vol. 1). (Berkeley, CA: University of California Press).
23. Parsons, T., 1937, The structure of social action (New York: McGrawHill).
24. Callon, M., and Blackwell, O., 2007, Actor-network theory. The politics of interventions (Oslo: Oslo Academic Press, 273–286).
25. Latour, B., 1996, On actor-network theory: A few clarifications. Soziale Welt, 47, 369–381.
26. Blumer, H., 1969, Symbolic interactionism: Perspective and method (Englewood Cliffs, NJ: Prentice-Hall).
27. Collins, R., 1984, The role of emotion in social structure. In Approaches to emotion (Hillsdale, NJ: Erlbaum, 385–396).
28. Blau, P. M., 1977, Inequality and heterogeneity: A primitive theory of social structure (Vol. 7). (New York: Free Press).
29. Brewster, K., 2013, Beyond classic symbolic interactionism: Towards a inter-sectional reading of George H. Mead's 'Mind, Self, and Society'. Conference Papers, 1–20 (Berkley, CA: American Sociological Association).
30. Blumer, H., 2004, George Herbert Mead and human conduct. (Landham, ML: Rowman Altamira).
31. Aboulafia, M., George Herbert Mead. The Stanford Encyclopedia of Philosophy Available at: https://plato.stanford.edu/archives/spr2020/entries/mead/ (Accessed May 15 2021).
32. Peirce, C. S., 2009, Writings of Charles S. Peirce: A chronological edition (Vol. 8). (Bloomington, IN: Indiana University Press, 1890–1892).
33. Rousi, R., 2013, From cute to content: User experience from a cognitive semiotic perspective. Jyväskylä studies in computing (Vol. 171). (Jyväskylä: University of Jyväskylä Press).
34. Saariluoma, P., and Rousi, R, 2015, Symbolic interactions: Towards a cognitive scientific theory of meaning in human technology interaction. Journal of Advances in Humanities, 3 (3), 310–324.
35. Frijda, N. H., 1993, Appraisal and beyond. Cognition & Emotion, 7(3–4), 225–231.
36. Clore, G. L., and Ortony, A., 2008, Appraisal theories: How cognition shapes affect into emotion. In Handbook of Emotions (New York, NY: The Guilford Press, 628–642).
37. Folkman, S., and Lazarus, R. S., 1984, Stress, appraisal, and coping. (New York: Springer Publishing Company).
38. Russell, J. A., 2003, Core affect and the psychological construction of emotion. Psychological Review, 110(1), 145.
39. Russell, J. A., 2009, Emotion, core affect, and psychological construction. Cognition and Emotion, 23(7), 1259–1283.
40. Brave, S., and Nass, C., 2007, Emotion in human-computer interaction. In The Human-Computer Interaction Handbook (Boca Raton, FL: CRC Press, 103–118).
41. Hekkert, P., 2006, Design aesthetics: Principles of pleasure in design. Psychology Science, 48(2), 157.

42. Williams, D. R., Patterson, M. E., Roggenbuck, J. W., and Watson, A. E., 1992, Beyond the commodity metaphor: Examining emotional and symbolic attachment to place. Leisure Sciences, 14(1), 29–46.

43. Tsai, S. P., 2005, Utility, cultural symbolism and emotion: A comprehensive model of brand purchase value. International Journal of Research in Marketing, 22(3), 277–291.

44. Latour, B., 2005, Reassembling the social: An introduction to actor-network-theory (Oxford: Oxford University Press).

45. Deleuze, G., and Guattari, F., 1988, A thousand plateaus: Capitalism and schizophrenia (London: Bloomsbury Publishing).

46. DeLanda, M., 2016, Assemblage theory (Edinburgh: Edinburgh University Press).

47. DeLanda, M., 2019, A new philosophy of society: Assemblage theory and social complexity (London: Bloomsbury Publishing).

48. Hall, S., 2003, Recent developments in theories of language and ideology: A critical note. In Culture, media, language (London: Routledge, 157–163).

49. Zizek, S., 2012, Organs without bodies: On Deleuze and consequences (London: Routledge).

50. Dreyfus, H. L., and Dreyfus, S. E., 2002, The challenge of Merleau-Ponty's phenomenology of embodiment for cognitive science (London: Routledge, 121–138).

51. Kinsbourne, M., and Jordan, J. S., 2009, Embodied anticipation: A neurodevelopmental interpretation. Discourse Processes, 46(2–3), 103–126.

52. Shusterman, R., 1994, Dewey on experience: Foundation or reconstruction? The Philosophical Forum, 26, 127–148.

53. Kirmayer, L. J., and Ramstead, M. J., 2017, 20 Embodiment and enactment in cultural psychiatry. In Embodiment, enaction, and culture: Investigating the constitution of the shared world (Cambridge, MA: MIT Press, 397).

54. Burns, T. R., and Engdahl, E., 1998, The social construction of consciousness. Part 1: collective consciousness and its socio-cultural foundations. Journal of Consciousness Studies, 5(1), 67–85.

55. IGI Global, 2021, What is Social Interaction. Available at: https://www.igi-global.com/dictionary/social-interaction/27371 (Accessed 19 April 2021).

56. Shusterman, R., 2012, Thinking through the body: Essays in somaesthetics (Cambridge: Cambridge University Press).

57. Shusterman, R., 2015, Somaesthetics. Encyclopedia of Human-Computer Interaction, 2nd Edition. Available at: https://www.interaction-design.org/literature/book/the-encyclopedia-of-human-computer-interaction-2nd-ed/somaesthetics (Accessed 2 May 2021).

58. Perlovsky, L., 2014, Aesthetic emotions, what are their cognitive functions? Frontiers in Psychology, 5, Article 98, 1–4. DOI: 10.3389/fpsyg.2014.00098

59. Kant, I., 1790, The critique of judgment, Translated by J. H. Bernard (Amherst, NY: Prometheus Books).

60. Baumgarten, H., 1992/1750, Aesthetica. In remembrance of things past: Music, autobiographical memory, and emotion. Advanced Consumer Research, 19, 613–620.

61. Gross, C. G., 1995, Aristotle on the brain. The Neuroscientist, 1(4), 245–250. DOI: 10.1177/107385849500100408
62. Bornstein, R. F., and D'agostino, P. R., 1992, Stimulus recognition and the mere exposure effect. Journal of Personality and Social Psychology, 63(4), 545–552.
63. Rousi, R., and Silvennoinen, J., 2018, Simplicity and the art of something more: A cognitive-semiotic approach to simplicity and complexity in human-technology interaction and design experience. Human Technology, 14 (1), 67–95. DOI: 10.17011/ht/urn.201805242752.
64. Chen, W., Shidujaman, M., Jin, J., and Ahmed, S. U., 2020, A methodological approach to create interactive art in artificial intelligence. In International Conference on Human-Computer Interaction (pp. 13–31). Springer, Cham.
65. Nass, C., 2010, The Man Who Lied to His Laptop. Available at: https://www.youtube.com/watch?v=lCuW2VOeS9Y (Accessed 20 April 2021).
66. Dartnall, T. H., 1993, AI, Creativity, Representational Redescription, Intentionality, Mental Life: An Emerging Picture. AAAI Technical Report SS-93-01. Available at: https://aaai.org/Papers/Symposia/Spring/1993/SS-93-01/SS-93-01-012.pdf (Accessed May 17 2021).
67. Rousi, R., 2018, Me, my bot and his other (robot) woman? Keeping your robot satisfied in the age of artificial emotion. Robotics, 7(3), 44.
68. McDermott, D., 1976, Artificial Intelligence Meets Natural Stupidity, SIGART Newsletter (of the Special Interest Group on Artificial Intelligence, of the Association for Computing Machinery). Available at: https://www.researchgate.net/publication/234784524_Artificial_Intelligence_meets_natural_stupidity (Accessed 16 May 2021).
69. Mitchell, M., 2021, Why AI Is Harder Than we Think. Available at: https://www.youtube.com/watch?v=WF_nm0axBzo (Accessed 15 May 2021).
70. Nehamas, A., 1975, Plato on the imperfection of the sensible world. American Philosophical Quarterly, 12(2), 105–117.
71. Buetow, S., and Wallis, K., 2019, The beauty in perfect imperfection. Journal of Medical Humanities, 40(3), 389–394.
72. Shelley, J., 2020, The concept of the aesthetic, The Stanford Encyclopedia of Philosophy (Winter 2020 Edition). Available at: https://plato.stanford.edu/archives/win2020/entries/aesthetic-concept/ (Accessed 19 April 2021).
73. Panagia, D., 2016, Ten Theses for an Aesthetics of Politics (Minnesota: University of Minnesota Press). Available at: https://manifold.umn.edu/read/ten-theses-for-an-aesthetics-of-politics/section/3d9c88b7-c366-4600-bb67-44a1b2c08faf (Accessed 10 May 2021).
74. IJsselsteijn, W. A., and Riva, G., 2003, Being there: The experience of presence in mediated environments. In New Technologies and Practices in Communication. Being There: Concepts, Effects and Measurements of User Presence in Synthetic Environments (Amsterdam: IOS Press, 3–16).
75. Hume, D., 1986, Enquiry concerning the principles of morals. In Enquiries concerning human understanding and concerning the principles of morals (Oxford: Oxford University Press). (Original work published in 1751).
76. Hatfield, G., 2002, Sense data and the philosophy of mind: Russell, James, and Mach. Principia: An International Journal of Epistemology, 6(2), 203–230.

77. Russell, B., 1913, The nature of sense-data - a reply to Dr. Dawes Hicks. Mind, 22(85), 76–81.
78. Reid, T., 2002, Essays on the intellectual powers of man - A Critical Edition. Edited by Derek R. Brookes. (Edinburgh: Edinburgh University Press). (Original work published in 1785).
79. Rancière, J., 2009, Aesthetics and its discontents (New York: Polity).
80. Landgrebe, J., and Smith, B., 2019, There is no general AI: why Turing machines cannot pass the Turing test. Available at: https://arxiv.org/abs/1906.05833 (Accessed 10 May 2021).
81. Natusch, B., 2013, Adding art to artifice in cyber conversations. In Stories in post-human cultures (Leiden: Brill, pp. 71–86).
82. Rousi, R. 2014, Unremarkable experiences – Designing the user experience of elevators. Swedish Design Research Journal, 11, 47–54.
83. Cahill, L., and McGaugh, J. L., 1998, Mechanisms of emotional arousal and lasting declarative memory. Trends in Neurosciences, 21(7), 294–299.
84. Larrain, A., and Haye, A., 2019, Self as an aesthetic effect. Frontiers in Psychology, 10, 1433.
85. Rudd, N. A., and Lennon, S. J., 2001, Body image: Linking aesthetics and social psychology of appearance. Clothing and Textiles Research Journal, 19(3), 120–133.
86. Crilly, N., Good, D., Matravers, D., and Clarkson, P. J., 2008, Design as communication: exploring the validity and utility of relating intention to interpretation. Design Studies, 29(5), 425–457.
87. Dennett, D., 2009, Intentional systems theory. The Oxford handbook of philosophy of mind. (Oxford: Oxford University Press, 339–350).
88. Gibson, J. J., 1979, The concept of affordances. Perceiving, acting, and knowing, 1. In The ecological approach to visual perception (Boston: Houghton Mifflin).
89. Norman, D. A., 2004, Affordances and design. Unpublished article, available online at: Available online at: https://jnd.org/affordances_and_design/ (Accessed 9 June 2021).
90. Norman, D. A., 1988, The psychology of everyday things. (New York: Basic books).
91. Jackson, S. W., 1994, Catharsis and abreaction in the history of psychological healing. Psychiatric Clinics of North America, 17(3), 471–491.
92. Aoki, B. Y., and Kimura, T., 2021, Sexuality and affection in the time of technological innovation: Artificial partners in the Japanese context. Religions, 12(5), 296.
93. Woodward, I., 2007, Understanding material culture (London: Sage).
94. Shidujaman, M., and Mi, H., 2018, "Which country are you from?" a cross-cultural study on greeting interaction design for social robots. In International Conference on Cross-Cultural Design (pp. 362–374). Springer, Cham.
95. Shidujaman, M., Mi, H., and Jamal, L., 2020, " I trust you more": A behavioral greeting gesture study on social robots for recommendation tasks. In 2020 International Conference on Image Processing and Robotics (ICIP) (IEEE, 1–5).

96. Dunbar, R., 2007, The social brain hypothesis and its relevance to social psychology. Evolution and the Social Mind: Evolutionary Psychology and Social Cognition. (Milton Park: Routledge/Taylor & Francis, 21–31).

97. Samani, H., Saadatian, E., Pang, N., Polydorou, D., Fernando, O. N. N., Nakatsu, R., and Koh, J. T. K. V., 2013, Cultural robotics: The culture of robotics and robotics in culture. International Journal of Advanced Robotic Systems, 10(12), 400.

98. Misselhorn, C., Pompe, U., and Stapleton, M., 2013, Ethical considerations regarding the use of social robots in the fourth age. GeroPsych: The Journal of Gerontopsychology and Geriatric Psychiatry, 26(2), 121–133.

99. Bourdieu, P. 1977, Structures and the habitus. In Outline of a theory of practice (Cambridge: Cambridge University Press, 72–95).

100. Beedie, C., Terry, P., and Lane, A., 2005, Distinctions between emotion and mood. Cognition & Emotion, 19(6), 847–878.

101. Peirce, C. S., 1998, Chance, love, and logic: Philosophical essays (Lincoln, NB: University of Nebraska Press).

102. Hay, J. C., Pick, H. L., and Ikeda, K., 1965, Visual capture produced by prism spectacles. Psychoneurological Science, 2, 215–216.

103. Rock, I., and Victor, J., 1964, Vision and touch: An experimentally created conflict between the two senses. Science, 143, 594–596.

104. Teghtsoonian, R., and Teghtsoonian, M., 1970, Two varieties of perceived length. Perception & Psychophysiology, 8, 389–392.

105. Fenko, A., Schifferstein, H. N., and Hekkert, P., 2010, Shifts in sensory dominance between various stages of user–product interactions. Applied Ergonomics, 41(1), 34–40.

106. Jaimes, B. N. O., 2019, The Effect of a Handshake on Psychosocial Stress, PhD thesis, San Jose State University.

107. Peled-Avron, L., Perry, A., and Shamay-Tsoory, S. G., 2016, The effect of oxytocin on the anthropomorphism of touch. Psychoneuroendocrinology, 66, 159–165.

108. Peck, J., 2011, Does touch matter? Insights from haptic research in marketing. In Sensory marketing (London: Routledge, 47–62).

109. Maville, J. A., Bowen, J. E., and Benham, G., 2008, Effect of healing touch on stress perception and biological correlates. Holistic Nursing Practice, 22(2), 103–110.

110. Spence, C., 2011, Crossmodal correspondences: A tutorial review. Attention, Perception, & Psychophysics, 73(4), 971–995.

111. Rupert, A. H., 2000, Tactile situation awareness system: Proprioceptive prostheses for sensory deficiencies. Aviation, Space, and Environmental Medicine, 71(9 Suppl), A92–A99.

112. Lara, A., 2015, Affect, heat and tacos. A speculative account of thermoception. The Senses and Society, 10(3), 275–297.

113. Pfaffmann, C., 1956, Taste and smell. Annual Review of Psychology, 7(1), 391–408.

114. Spinella, M., 2002, A relationship between smell identification and empathy. International Journal of Neuroscience, 112(6), 605–612.

115. Thomas, D. L., and Diener, E., 1990, Memory accuracy in the recall of emotions. Journal of Personality and Social Psychology, 59(2), 291.
116. Willander, J., and Larsson, M., 2006, Smell your way back to childhood: Autobiographical odor memory. Psychonomic Bulletin & Review, 13(2), 240–244.
117. Korsmeyer, C., 2015, Making sense of taste. (Ithaca, NY: Cornell University Press).
118. Neely, E., Walton, M., and Stephens, C., 2014, Young people's food practices and social relationships. A thematic synthesis. Appetite, 82, 50–60.
119. Spence, C., 2015, Just how much of what we taste derives from the sense of smell?. Flavour, 4(1), 1–10.
120. Meier, B. P., Moeller, S. K., Riemer-Peltz, M., and Robinson, M. D., 2012, Sweet taste preferences and experiences predict prosocial inferences, personalities, and behaviors. Journal of Personality and Social Psychology, 102(1), 163–174.

CHAPTER 3

Cyber-Physical System for Automated Service of Restaurant Visitors in Conditions of Mandatory Wearing of Masks

Anton Saveliev, Irina Vatamaniuk,
Maksim Letenkov, and Roman Lakolev

St. Petersburg Federal Research Center of the Russian Academy of Sciences (SPC RAS), St. Petersburg Institute for Informatics and Automation of the Russian Academy of Sciences, St. Petersburg, Russia

CONTENTS

DOI: 10.1201/9781003195061-3

3.1 INTRODUCTION

Cyber-physical systems aimed at interacting with the environment are widely used in solving modern complex problems, for example when designing a 'smart' city, which implies a single system that includes law enforcement, and management of the transport system, and management of energy resources, water supply and health care [1–4]. Also, cyber-physical systems allow solving problems of servicing people [5]. In direct interaction with a person, such systems are called socio-cyberphysical. The use of cyber-physical systems can extend to the catering sector. This allows you to significantly reduce costs due to the absence of cashiers and the presence of an automated kitchen, as well as reduce the number of contacts between people. But this solution is not universal, since it may be necessary to issue orders to the client on the table, and while solving this problem, the following problems may arise determining the location of a person in the room, determining his position (standing or sitting), building an optimal route and registering obstacles that have arisen.

In addition, considering the high rates of spread of the new coronavirus infection COVID-19 [6], as well as the established measures to curb the growth of the number of infected citizens, consisting in the need to wear personal protective equipment [7], it is worth noting that there is a critical need for the development of specialised biometric systems; identification capable of recognition in conditions of partial overlapping of the user's face.

To implement a system capable of solving such problems, you need both sensors and video cameras, as well as the corresponding software. The programs of such systems may include machine and deep learning algorithms, which make it possible to process large amounts of data in the form of a stream of images, data on the location of people and their status.

The purpose of this work is to develop a socio-cyberphysical system for tracking people in a restaurant complex, which, using a robotic system and machine learning algorithms, will solve the above problems. For this, algorithms were developed for identifying people by face while wearing masks, tracking people in the premises of the restaurant complex and determining the status of a person to build a route for delivering orders depending on where the person is. Thus, the developed human tracking system will allow the robotic system to transmit all the necessary information to build a path to the person who made a certain order, and to register dynamic obstacles on the paved route to change the trajectory of the robot.

3.2 DESCRIPTION OF THE DEVELOPED APPROACH

Consider the formulation of the problem, the proposed solution and the developed algorithm for tracking a person in a restaurant complex. It is required to solve the problem of tracking people in the premises of a restaurant complex for the navigation of a robotic system. This task is broken down into the following sub-tasks:

1. Detection of the human body in the frame.

2. Detection of a person's face in the frame.

3. Checking the presence of a mask and identifying a person by face.

4. Tracking the movements of a person in the territory of the restaurant complex.

5. Assigning a completed and paid order to a person.

6. Determining the status of a person (walking/standing, sitting, waiting for an order, the order has not been placed) and his location at a certain point in time for the delivery of the order by a robotic device or considering his position to build and correct the constructed route.

7. Exclusion from the list of tracked people when a person leaves the restaurant complex.

Thus, it is necessary to develop such algorithms that, when a person enters a restaurant complex, will make it possible to detect the person's face, check the presence of a mask on him, identify him and start tracking. It is also necessary that the algorithm allows assigning an order number to the person who made and paid for it. In addition, the developed surveillance system must track the location of a person, that is be able to localise him, as well as determine the status of each person for the delivery of an order by a robotic device and correct planning of the trajectory of his movement.

3.3 HUMAN DETECTION AND IDENTIFICATION

The process of detecting and identifying a person should take place at the entrance to the premises. Thus, it is necessary to equip the entrance room so that it is possible to both carry out detection and identification and start the process of tracking a person.

To solve this problem, it is proposed to use two observation systems:

1. A surveillance system consisting of one camera, the field of view of which will cover the front door, which can detect the faces of incoming people and identify them by their faces.

2. A surveillance system consisting of a group of dome cameras placed on the ceiling to track human movements between the premises of the restaurant complex.

By analysing the frames received from the camera included in the first surveillance system, a check is made for the presence of a mask on the face, face recognition and assignment of a unique ID. Thanks to the analysis of the frames received from the cameras of the second surveillance system, the person with the ID assigned to him is tracked.

Further, the global coordinate system will mean the coordinate system of a specific room in the restaurant complex, in which the coordinates of each object are determined in metres. Under the local coordinate system – the coordinate system of the image received from the camera, in which the position of the object on the frame is determined in pixels.

It is proposed to use an RGBD camera as a camera designed to identify people by face. The RGB (Red Green Blue) stream is used for identification, and the D (Distance) stream is used to transform coordinates into the global coordinate system of the entrance room.

Each person monitored by surveillance systems is an object and has several attributes. In the case of tracking a person by the first surveillance system, the person has the following attributes:

1. $(x_1^1, y_1^1), (x_2^1, y_2^1)$ are the coordinates of the position of the upper-left and lower-right corners of the frame into which the person's face is selected (in pixels) on the frame.

2. z is the distance from the camera to the person's face.

3. ID – unique identifier.

Figure 3.1 shows examples of frames received from cameras of the first and second surveillance systems.

In the case of tracking a person by the second surveillance system, the person has the following attributes:

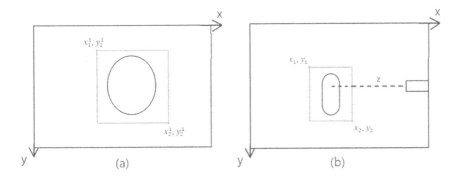

FIGURE 3.1 (a) An example of a frame received from the camera of the first surveillance system (black outer square is the frame border, oval is a person's face, the green center square is a frame that limits the detected face). (b) An example of a frame received from the dome camera of the second surveillance system in the entrance group (the rectangle on the right is the camera of the first surveillance system, the dashed line is the distance z from the camera to the person, the oval is the human body).

1. $(x_1^2, y_1^2), (x_2^2, y_2^2)$ are the coordinates of the upper-left and lower-right corners of the frame into which the tracked person is highlighted (in metres).

2. ID – unique identifier.

3. $(x_1, y_1), (x_2, y_2)$ are the coordinates of the upper-left and lower-right corners of the frame into which the tracked person is selected (in pixels).

4. 'State status' takes on the values 'Sitting' or 'Standing/Running' (the value during initialisation is 'Standing/Running').

5. 'Order status' takes on the values 'No order' or 'There is an order' (the value during initialisation is 'No order').

Since the coordinates of the object for the first observation system are expressed in pixels, and for the second – in metres, then at first the coordinates of the object of each person in pixels will be transmitted to the second observation system. The resulting position of a person in the local coordinate system of the dome camera, expressed in pixels, must be converted to a position in the global metric coordinate system.

Thus, each tracked object has the coordinates of the object in the global coordinate system and a unique identifier assigned to it as attributes.

Tracking of a person by surveillance systems is carried out using tracking algorithms.

During the operation of the second surveillance system, the tracking algorithm may malfunction tracking the person. This can result in any other object in the frame around which the tracked person with the attached ID is supposed to be. The occurrence of such cases must be registered, and the lost unique identifier of a person must be re-assigned.

To register these errors, it is proposed to process the image from the dome camera with a neural network model for detecting people every N frames. During processing, it is possible to identify people whose tracking has been violated. A sign of an error while tracking a person is the absence of a frame that limits a person to the tracking algorithm.

Next, you need to implement the possibility of placing and paying for the order. For this, it is proposed to use a payment terminal. If a person pays for an order at a certain point in time, the automated system receives information that payment for the order was made in terminal No. X, therefore, now, there is a person who made the order at this terminal. With the help of dome cameras located on the ceiling, it is determined which ID is at the terminal. The order number will be assigned to the person who is currently at the terminal number X.

To exclude the possibility of finding two people opposite the terminal at the same distance, it is proposed to place a railing near the payment terminal. This will allow you to uniquely identify the person who paid for the order. When the order is ready, a robotic device picks it up from a special rack and delivers it to a person. Next, consider the developed algorithms for tracking a person in a restaurant complex.

3.4 FACE MASK DETECTION

For recognition of users in conditions of partial overlapping of faces by means of personal protective equipment, a neural network model of deep learning FaceNet [8] was chosen as the initial model, a distinctive feature of which is high recognition accuracy, as well as work in real time. The generalised architecture of the FaceNet neural network model is shown in Figure 3.2.

Within the framework of this generalised architecture, one can distinguish between a batch input layer, a deep learning block that includes a basic deep learning model, and an L2 regularisation block (L2). In this block, the implementation of GoogleNet, based on the Inception-Resenet-v1 architecture [9], is used as a reference model for deep learning.

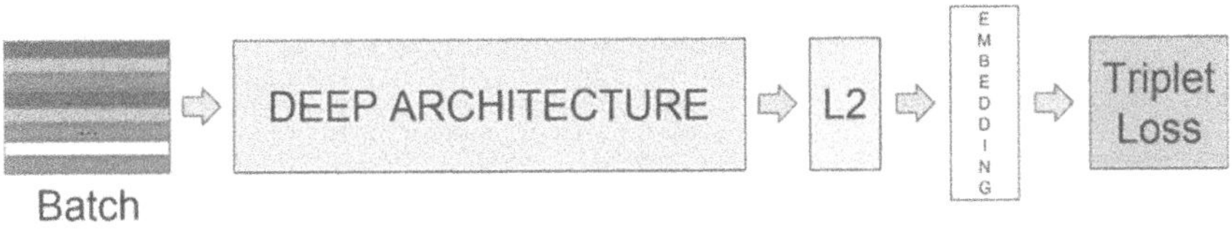

FIGURE 3.2   Generalised architecture of the FaceNet neural network model [8].

Interaction with a deep learning block within the FaceNet model is carried out according to the principle of interaction with a black box.

To reduce the spatial dimension, GoogleNet uses convolution operations with 1×1 filters. Using these operations allows you to reduce the number of channels while maintaining the remaining characteristics (height and width) of the input data. Thus, it is possible to convert a $256 \times 256 \times 3$ RGB image to a $256 \times 256 \times 1$ image by means of the inception module. Convolution operations 3×3, 5×5, 7×7, as well as max-pooling layers allow to reduce the dimension of the processed data.

Within the framework of the FaceNet neural network model, the loss function is defined as the element-wise sum of the values of the triplet loss function and the L2 regularisation function. In the process of training the model, the triplet loss function seeks on the one hand, to minimise the distances between each estimated image (anchor) and positive with respect to the estimated image instances, and on the other hand, to maximise the distances between each estimated image and negative with respect to the estimated image instances. This process is implemented for each class included in the training sample. The L2-regularisation function, in turn, is used to combat model overfitting.

To train the model, the VGGFace2 dataset was used, supplemented with a set of generated semi-synthetic images containing images of human faces, partially hidden by personal protective equipment. The formation of the corresponding images was carried out based on the initial data from the VGGFace2 set as follows. In each image, areas of the face and their key points were detected. Distorted images were aligned using affine transformations. Thus, an intermediate dataset was obtained, consisting of aligned RGB images of selected user faces with a size of 160×160 pixels (Figure 3.3, top row). This stage of data preparation was performed using Multi-task CNN (MTCNN) [10].

At the next stage of data preparation, the generation of semi-synthetic images of human faces with artificially imposed personal protective equipment was directly carried out. For the formation of the corresponding set

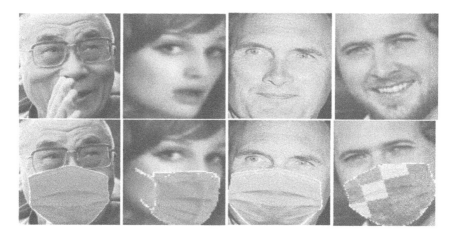

FIGURE 3.3 Results of generating semisynthetic data samples based on the aligned VGGFace2 dataset using the MaskTheFace package.

of images, the MaskTheFace package was used [11]. MaskTheFace provides a range of personal protective equipment templates, most of which are medical masks, and allows to customise not only the colour of the template but also the filling texture. The results of this stage of preparing the training dataset are shown in Figure 3.3, bottom row.

Thus, for each image from the VGGFace2 set, a version with personal protective equipment superimposed on the face was generated while maintaining the original aligned image. Images that did not pass the augmentation process were not included in the extended version of the VGGFace2 dataset.

3.5 HUMAN TRACKING ALGORITHM

The human tracking process begins by capturing a video stream from an RGBD camera in the entrance group. The algorithm for capturing the video stream and identification is shown in Figure 3.4. For the set C we will take the set of people detected by the RGBD camera, and for the set P – the set of identified people by the RGBD camera.

First, the video stream is captured from the RGBD camera. Further, with each frame update, all faces in the frame are detected and the set C is filled. After that, for each found face c_i, the coordinates of the face position are determined by the D and RGB streams. Then the face is identified. The identified element of the set C is added to the set of identified people P as p_i.

In order for a surveillance system consisting of dome cameras to be able to assign an ID to a person, which was obtained using an RGBD camera, it is necessary to transform the coordinates of the person's position (x_1^1, y_1^1),

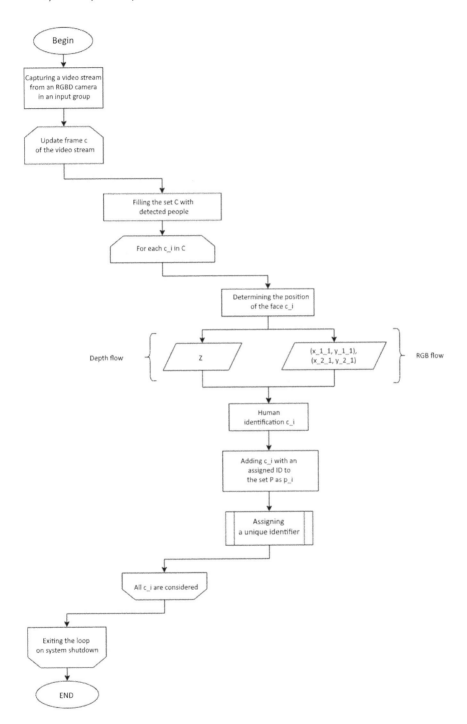

FIGURE 3.4 **Algorithm for capturing a video stream from an RGBD camera and identifying people.**

(x_2^1, y_2^1), z in the RGBD camera coordinate system to the coordinates of the person's position (x_1^2, y_1^2), (x_2^2, y_2^2) in the global metric coordinate system.

First, there is a transformation (x_1^1, y_1^1), (x_2^1, y_2^1), z to (x_1, y_1), (x_2, y_2), where each coordinate is determined in pixels relative to the origin of the image obtained from cameras. Next, it is necessary to transform the position of a person in the local coordinate system, expressed in pixels, into the position of a person in the global metric coordinate system (x_1^2, y_1^2), (x_2^2, y_2^2).

To convert a person's coordinates from a local coordinate system to a global one, you need to know:

1. Distance from floor to dome camera

2. Camera angle

3. The resolution at which the camera is shooting

Figure 3.5 shows a diagram for converting a position point from pixels to metres.

When installing the dome camera indoors, it is necessary to determine the height of its position in metres h and the angle of view α. Based on these values, the remaining variables are calculated by elementary geometric transformations. The value of c in pixels is known, let us determine

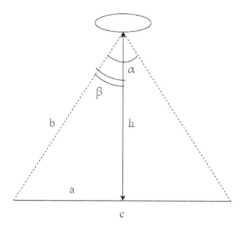

FIGURE 3.5 Scheme for converting a position point from pixels to metres (oval – dome camera, dotted lines – boundaries of the camera's field of view).

the coefficient of transformation of coordinates from pixels to metres along the abscissa axis:

$$\gamma_x = \frac{2a}{c} = \frac{\sqrt{h^2 - \left(\dfrac{h}{\cos\left(\dfrac{a}{2}\right)}\right)^2}}{c} \qquad (3.1)$$

To transform coordinates from the local coordinate system to the global one, it is necessary to multiply the coordinate along the abscissa axis by the γ_x coefficient. The determination of the transformation coefficient of coordinates along the abscissa axis γ_y is similar, with the only exception that the value of c changes.

At the next step, a unique identifier obtained from the analytical part of the first video surveillance system is assigned to the person detected by the neural network model using the cameras of the second video surveillance system. The algorithm for assigning a unique identifier is shown in Figure 3.6. For the set L, we take the set of people detected by the dome camera of the second surveillance system.

Consider the algorithm for assigning a unique identifier. At the first stage, the transformation (x_1^1, y_1^1), (x_2^1, y_2^1), z to (x_1, y_1), (x_1, y_1) occurs, where each coordinate is expressed in pixels relative to the starting point of the image (upper-left corner). Next, the obtained coordinates are converted from the local image coordinate system to the global metric coordinate system (x_1^2, y_1^2), (x_2^2, y_2^2).

An object that has coordinates in the global metric coordinate system is assigned a unique identifier obtained using an RGBD camera as an ID attribute. After assigning a unique ID to each element of the set L, the stream from dome cameras is processed. The algorithm for capturing a video stream from dome cameras and the process of tracking people is shown in Figure 3.7. For the set A, we take the set of unidentified people detected by the dome camera of the second surveillance system.

When processing a frame from a captured video stream, all people are detected, and the sets P and A are filled. Identified people are added to set P, and unidentified people are added to set A. If the cardinality of set A is greater than zero, then in the process of tracking someone's ID was lost.

Next, each element of the set L is analysed, the algorithm of which is shown in Figure 3.8.

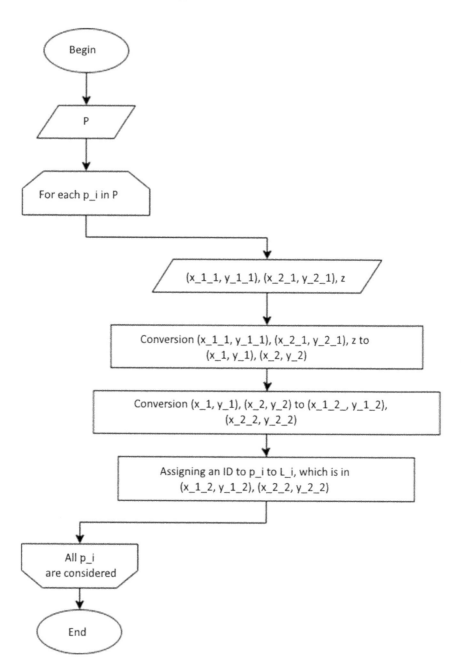

FIGURE 3.6 Algorithm for assigning a unique identifier.

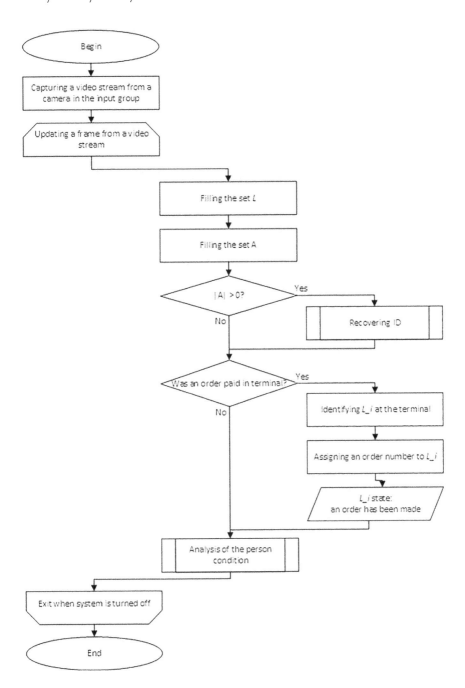

FIGURE 3.7 Algorithm for capturing a video stream from dome cameras and tracking a person.

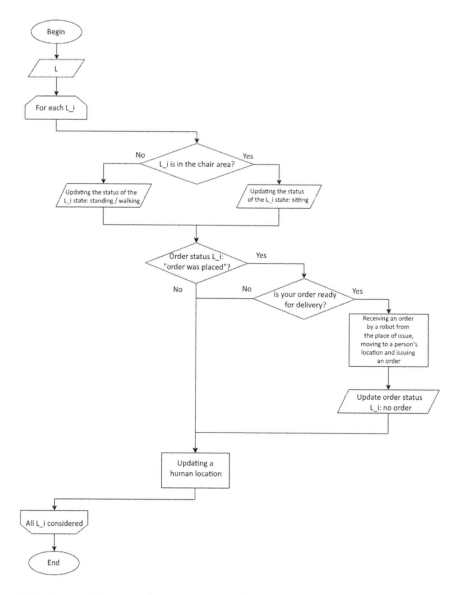

FIGURE 3.8 **Algorithm for analysing people observed from dome cameras.**

For each element of the set L, its state is determined. This allows for better route planning for the delivery of the order by the robotic means. If a person is in the sitting area, it means that with a high probability he is sitting, and this element of the set receives the status of the 'sitting' state, and otherwise it has the status of 'standing/walking'. If a person is sitting, then he is a static obstacle, which will be considered when planning the route.

If a person is standing or walking, then he is a dynamic obstacle for the robot, overcoming which is made directly now of movement of the robot.

After this step, it is determined whether the person has the 'Order was made' status. If it has this status, then the state of readiness of the order for issue is checked. If the order is ready, the robot picks it up from the place of issue and delivers it to the person. After the order has been delivered, the person's order status changes to 'No order'. After that, the location of the person is updated.

There are also cases where the size of the room can exceed the dome camera's field of view. In such a situation, it is possible to implement a surveillance system with multiple dome cameras that cover the entire room. Then, to implement tracking of people, it is proposed to divide the room into sectors, to each of which a camera observing it is attached.

To track the movements of a person between the sectors of the premises of the restaurant complex, it is proposed to place the dome cameras in such a way that the viewing angles of the cameras of the neighbouring sectors intersect. When a person moves to the edge of the sector, the camera from the sector into which the person is moving registers the appearance of the person and receives an identification number using information received from the dome camera from the sector from which the person is moving.

A restaurant complex can consist of several large rooms, divided into sectors and having their own global coordinate systems. In this case, it is proposed to place a group of dome cameras in each room. Then, to localise a person on the territory of a restaurant complex, it is necessary to know both his coordinates in the global coordinate system and the unique number of the room itself.

It is also possible that a person leaves the restaurant complex without making an order. In this case, the person's ID will be lost from the tracking. In addition, when tracking all people, a person with a lost ID will not be present in the system, that is the set A will be empty, therefore, the person left the restaurant complex, and his further tracking will be stopped.

3.6 SIMULATION RESULTS

3.6.1 User Service Process Modelling

To test the performance of the developed algorithm for tracking a person on the territory of a restaurant complex, we will conduct a simulation in the Gazebo environment. Gazebo environment is a free open-source simulator with a physics engine that allows testing the developed systems and robotic devices in scenarios as close as possible to reality [12].

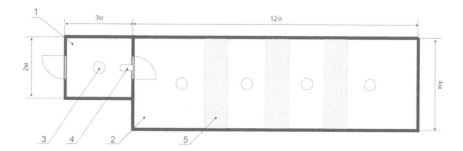

FIGURE 3.9 Simplified layout of the restaurant complex (1 – entrance group, 2 – main room, 3 – dome camera located on the ceiling, 4 – RGBD camera, 5 – area with intersecting fields of view of neighbouring cameras).

We will develop a simplified layout of the restaurant complex, which consists of an entrance group and a main room (Figure 3.9).

Using the Building Editor in the Gazebo environment, as well as adding a three-dimensional animated model of a person to the scene, we will create a simplified model of the restaurant complex (Figure 3.10). The dome cameras are located at a height of 3 metres, and the RGBD camera is located at a height of 2 metres.

At the first stage, it is necessary to detect a person's face and identify it. In the simulated environment, there is a simplified model of a person, so the use of neural network models for face detection and identification is impossible. These experiments were performed separately (see next section). The selection of the face area when the human model enters the territory of the restaurant complex is done manually. Then, using the RGBD camera's depth stream, the distance to the face of the human model is determined. Further, information about the distance to the face is transmitted

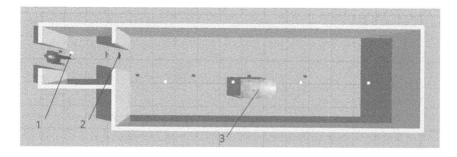

FIGURE 3.10 Simplified model of a restaurant complex (1 – dome camera, 2 – RGBD camera, 3 – 3D table model).

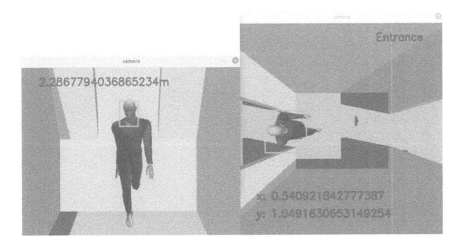

FIGURE 3.11 Human model detection and localisation (left – view from an RGBD camera, right – view from a dome camera located on the ceiling).

to the dome camera of the second surveillance system, located on the ceiling of the entrance group, with the help of which a person is detected and localised on the territory of the restaurant complex, that is his coordinates and the room in which he is located are determined (Figure 3.11). Thus, at any time it is possible to localise a person on the territory of the restaurant complex.

The right image of Figure 3.11 shows a vertical line. It marks the boundary of the entrance room. If the coordinate of the person on the abscissa axis exceeds the threshold value, then the person has left the entrance room and is currently in the main room 'Room 1' (Figure 3.12).

In the case when the human model has moved from the entrance room to the main room, information about this is transmitted to the neighbouring dome camera, in the field of view of which the human model has moved. Then the emerging person is detected, localised and tracked (Figure 3.12 [right]). In Figure 3.12 [right], the vertical line on the left is the border of the 'Room 1' room, and the vertical line on the right is the border of the area where the fields of view intersect with the adjacent camera.

When the human model is moved to the area of intersection of the fields of view of two cameras, information from the analytical part of the dome camera, from the field of view of which the human model is moving, is transmitted to the analytical part of the dome camera, into the field of view of which it moves. Thus, tracking by the analytical part of the first chamber stops, and the second one starts (Figure 3.13).

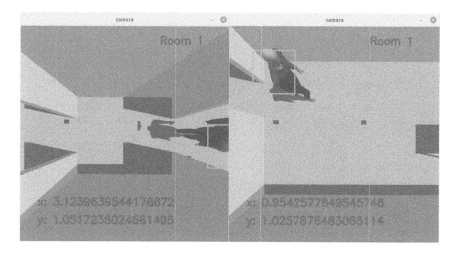

FIGURE 3.12 (left) Localisation of a person when leaving the entrance room. (right) Detection, localisation, and tracking of a model of a person when entering the main room.

By default, the human model has the 'Standing/Walking' status. If the human model is in the table seats (Figure 3.14, yellow [light] rectangle), the person's status changes to 'Sitting', or 'Sitting', as shown in Figure 3.14.

If the person model leaves the restaurant complex, tracking stops and the item is removed from the set of tracked people.

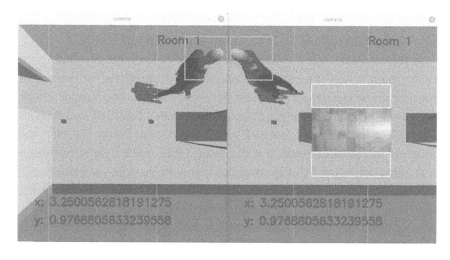

FIGURE 3.13 Tracking a human model when moving to the area of intersection of the fields of view of two cameras (white rectangles – the area of the table seats).

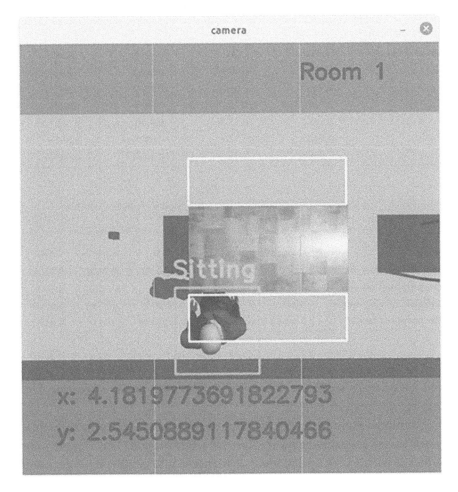

FIGURE 3.14 Changing a person's status to 'Sitting'.

3.6.2 Testing the Face Mask Recognition Process

Training and validation of the selected FaceNet neural network model was carried out on the extended Masked VGGFace2 dataset, which includes 5,830,200 images. Training (4,951,566 images) and deferred control samples (878,634 images) were formed. The neural network model was trained using the cross-validation procedure. Cross-validation made it possible to determine the number of model training epochs at which the smallest value of the loss function would be achieved without retraining the model. The best results are achieved, as a rule, in the 8th era of training. The average values of the Accuracy metric obtained when evaluating models trained using cross-validation are shown in Table 3.1.

TABLE 3.1   Values of the Accuracy Metric Obtained by Evaluating Models Trained Using Cross-Validation

Subset of Images	Accuracy	Loss	Precision	Recall
No. 1	0.9413	0.3358	0.8903	0.8903
No. 2	0.9418	0.3341	0.8912	0.8912
No. 3	0.9372	0.3544	0.8830	0.8829
No. 4	0.9412	0.3378	0.8901	0.8901
No. 5	0.9427	0.3265	0.8927	0.8927
Mean	0.9408	0.3377	0.8895	0.8894

TABLE 3.2   The Results of Evaluating the Accuracy of Model Predictions on Test Samples from the Original and Extended Datasets

Model	Delayed Test Fetch (Model)	AAc	AP	AR
Original FaceNet **model**	VGGFace2	0.999987	0.9354	0.9306
The proposed model	VGGFace2	0.999992	0.9635	0.9606
Original FaceNet **model**	Masked VGGFace2	0.999930	0.7649	0.6556
The proposed model	Masked VGGFace2	0.999989	0.9488	0.9457

AAc (average accuracy over classes), AP (average precision over classes) and AR (average recall over classes) [13] were used as target metrics. The results are shown in Table 3.2.

The model trained on the original dataset showed an unsatisfactory result in the experiment on the test set from Masked VGGFace2 – the values of AP and AR quality metrics turned out to be 25% lower on average. The proposed solution demonstrates the best results both on the test sample, including masked faces, and on the test sample without them.

3.7 CONCLUSION

During this study, the problem of developing algorithms for recognising and tracking the location of people on the territory of a restaurant complex under the conditions of mandatory wearing of masks was studied. In particular, the neural network models of detection, tracking and identification were studied, as well as the ways of their application in the developed socio-cyber-physical system were investigated. In addition, a selection of models for use in the developed system was made.

The robotic system used on the territory of the restaurant complex receives information about the coordinates of a person and his status, and then uses it both to build a route and to deliver an order to a person.

The developed solution for face recognition in a mask demonstrated significantly higher quality indicators of face recognition both without masks (AP = 0.9635) and with masks (AP = 0.9488). In comparison with the original model, the increase in the recognition accuracy by the AP metric was more than 24% in the first case and about 3% in the second.

The main advantage of the proposed visitor tracking system is its versatility. The developed method can be applied in restaurant complexes with one small or large room, and with several rooms of various sizes. When implementing the developed algorithm in practice, various variations of the location of the cameras are also possible, considering the peculiarities of the layout of the premises.

The selected neural network models of detection, identification and tracking made it possible to achieve a high speed of the system, which makes it possible to use it on mobile robotic devices.

The simulation results show that the developed method of tracking a person on the territory of a restaurant complex has broad application prospects. The developed solutions can serve as a basis for automated delivery of an order to a visitor using a mobile robot and correct planning of the trajectory of its movement [14].

REFERENCES

1. CDTOCenter. Smart nation, or what is interesting about Singapore's digital transformation experience? https://habr.com/ru/company/cdtocenter/blog/530154/ (accessed November 26, 2020), in russ.
2. Toshiba. 2019. Cyber-physical systems in the modern world. https://habr.com/ru/company/toshibarus/blog/438262/ (accessed January 26, 2020), in russ.
3. Fomin, N. A., Meshcheryakov, R. V., Iskhakov, A. Y., & Gromov, Y. Y. 2021. Smart city: Cyber-physical systems modeling features. In Society 5.0: Cyberspace for Advanced Human-Centered Society. Springer, Cham, 75–90.
4. Desnitsky, V. A., Chechulin, A. A., Kotenko, I. V., Levshun, D. S., & Kolomeec, M. V. 2016. Combined design technique for secure embedded devices exemplified by a perimeter protection system. SPIIRAS Proceedings 5:48 5–31. DOI: 10.15622/sp.48.1
5. Vatamaniuk I., & Iakovlev R. 2020. Personalization of user interaction with corporate information providing system based on analysis of user preferences. IEEE 10th International Conference on Intelligent Systems (IS). IEEE, 392–398. DOI: 10.1109/IS48319.2020.9199955
6. Spinelli A., & Pellino G. 2020. COVID-19 pandemic: perspectives on an unfolding crisis. The British Journal of Surgery 107:7 785–787. DOI: 10.1002/bjs.11627
7. Feng, S., Shen, C., Xia, N., Song, W., Fan, M., & Cowling, B. J. 2020. Rational use of face masks in the COVID-19 pandemic. The Lancet Respiratory Medicine 8:5 434–436.

8. Schroff F., Kalenichenko D., Philbin J., & FaceNet. 2015. A unified embedding for face recognition and clustering. Proceedings of the IEEE conference on computer vision and pattern recognition 815–823.

9. Szegedy, C., Ioffe, S., Vanhoucke, V., & Alemi, A. 2017. Inception-v4, inception-ResNet and the impact of residual connections on learning. Proceedings of the AAAI Conference on Artificial Intelligence 31:1.

10. Zhang, K., Zhang, Z., Li, Z., & Qiao, Y. 2016. Joint face detection and alignment using multitask cascaded convolutional networks. IEEE Signal Processing Letters 23:10 1499–1503.

11. Computer vision-based script "Mask the Face". 2020. https://github.com/aqeelanwar/MaskTheFace (accessed February 1, 2020).

12. Gazebo. Beginner: GUI. http://gazebosim.org/tutorials?cat=guided_b&tut=guided_b2 (accessed February 10, 2020).

13. Padilla R., Netto S. L., & da Silva E. A. B. 2020. A survey on performance metrics for object-detection algorithms. International Conference on Systems, Signals and Image Processing (IWSSIP) 237–242.

14. Ryumin D., Kagirov I., Axyonov A., Pavlyuk N., Saveliev A., Kipyatkova I., Zelezny M., Mporas I., & Karpov A. 2020. A multimodal user interface for an assistive robotic shopping cart. Electronics 9:12 2093. DOI: https://doi.org/10.3390/electronics9122093

CHAPTER 4

Low-Cost Delivery and Telepresence Robot for the COVID-19 Crisis

Arnon Jumlongkul

Mae Fah Luang University, Chiang Rai, Thailand

CONTENTS

4.1 INTRODUCTION

To minimize the spread of COVID-19, 'social distancing' has become a major necessity. To provide social distancing, the Centers for Disease Control and Prevention (CDC) has recommended everyone to maintain at least 6 ft between themselves and others, to avoid groups and stay out

DOI: 10.1201/9781003195061-4

of crowded places [1]. An increasingly used solution for the creation of social distancing is healthcare robotics. Emerging technologies in medical robots have included robots for stock control, cleaning, delivery, sterilisation, surgery, telepresence, as companions, cognitive therapy, rehabilitation and also humanoid robots [2]. For medical logistics tasks, delivery robots have been chosen to help prevent dissemination of COVID-19. Some hospitals have requested automated transport vehicles, which can collect and deliver any materials, are easy to load and unload by healthcare personnel, as well as be programmed for specific locations for pick-up and delivery. Delivery or service robots should be intuitive to control, to send an object to a destination, easy to command via touch screens and even detect and avoid obstacles [3].

When considering telecommunication between healthcare personnel and COVID-19 patients, who by necessity must stay in a quarantine ward or negative pressure isolation room, a teleoperated or telepresence robot is needed for this mission. The main concept of telepresence robotic function is to establish a meeting which is not limited only to a conference room, by amalgamating communication with a video-conference system, also called mobile robotic telepresence (MRP) system. MRP systems generally consist of a web camera, amplifier, LCD screen, two-way communication and ideally also have mobility. In healthcare systems, telepresence robots have been used in many areas, for instance, postoperative care units, intensive care units (ICU), anatomy laboratories, in surgical teaching and elderly in place facilities [4]. Therefore, the emergence of telepresence and delivery robots is an appropriate technology for the present COVID-19 crisis and the 'new normal' era. However, in Thailand, we also lack an optimum prototype of a telepresence system amalgamated with a delivery robot that can provide an economic dual transportation and communication machine to support social distancing in a hospital. Almost all delivery robot prototypes cannot be incorporated with an aluminium cart. Sometimes a mechanical system must be attached to a cart with drilling screws, bolts, or cutting some parts of a cart, then, an existing cart will be useless if the user needs to remove a cart for other applications.

During this COVID-19 pandemic situation, many companies have tried to apply automated solutions to support their healthcare workers against viral exposure, for example using fixed-based and mobile manipulators to perform tasks, developing wheeled mobile robots, flying mobile robots, legged mobile robots, wearable robots for measurement of body signals, exoskeletal robots for strengthening and rehabilitation, etc. The mechanical designs of human–robot interaction modality have also included telerobotics (e.g. the da Vinci Surgical Robot), collaborative robots (e.g. semiautonomous ultrasound scans), autonomous robots (e.g. UV sterilisation robots), wearable robots for measuring body signals and physical activity of patients and also social robots, like humanoids, respectively. To manage medical infection control tasks, telerobots have inevitably become perceived as leading actors [5]. One of the robotics in global COVID-19 healthcare management is a serving robot, which is deployed to supply food, drugs, beverages and laundries to COVID-19 patients in many Chinese as well as Singapore hospitals [6]. Due to the rapid outbreak of COVID-19, in China, 14 robots were deployed in the field hospital named Wuhan Hongshan Stadium. They were used to deliver drugs and food, disinfect, measure patient temperature and entertain patients. Like in Italy, the Tommy robot is used to communicate to patients visually and also acoustically [7]. However, because of budgetary restraints, lockdown policies and technology shortfalls, to design and build an intelligent healthcare robot in developing countries within a short period will be an unlikely occurrence. Even though these robots can provide social distancing, by the way, they also need the best Wi-Fi system within a building, which has not been adequate in remote areas, especially in many rural community hospitals in developing countries.

So to summarize, the purpose of this article was to attempt to design and fabricate a healthcare robot for use against COVID-19 that uses an optimum technology for low and middle income countries, to provide dual functions of telepresence and delivery operations, that is easy to assemble, similar to a general hospital cart, easy to clean with standard anti-microbial agents and that also can support effective telecommunications both inside and outside a hospital building.

4.2 MATERIALS AND METHODS

Some considerations, already mentioned in this article, were separated into two areas as follows:

4.2.1 Delivery Function and Circuit Architecture

The machine concept is centred on usefulness, low-cost and compatibility with most hospital carts of varying sizes. Therefore, an optimum design of healthcare robotics should be able to be assembled such that existing carts can be easily mounted to and removed from the new compact robot without drilling for screws or bolts. The machinery control parts of the robot were designed using SolidWorks 2017 software. The structural base frame was constructed from steel sprayed with rust-proof colour. The upper part of the base frame can be adjusted according to the size of a cart. This robot consists of 4 PVC caster wheels, which can be turned through 360°. The driving and steering systems use dual 24 V 150 W DC motors, driving the pneumatic tired wheels via a worm gear NMRV030, which can drive the left and right wheel independently. The battery system consists of dual 12 V 45 Ah Lithium batteries, joined in a series, for both delivery and telepresence functions, the batteries being housed in stainless steel boxes. To prevent driving system damage, a linear 100 mm 24 V DC actuator motor is used to elevate the pair of driving wheels free from the ground when the electric system is off.

The electrical circuit is mainly composed of two sets of voltage protection circuits, which cause cut off when the voltage drops below 23.8 V, and switches on when the voltage is above 23.9 V. The remote-control system receiver was designed to support 10 channels. The DC motors are controlled by a pulse width modulation (PWM) system, which receives signals from the remote control, allowing two channels for each driving wheel as well as another set for the linear motor. A step-up boost converter, which can convert the voltage from 24 V to 48 V, was provided for a fitted surveillance camera. All electronic parts were housed in a waterproof electrical control box. The electrical circuit of the driving system is shown in Figure 4.1.

A waterproof switch box houses two DC voltmeters, with LCD voltage displays, one for each of the functions of transportation and communication. The entire structure was designed to allow protection of the electronics from disinfectant cleaning solutions. To replicate and build this model, the robot drawing is shown in Figure 4.2. The dimensions of the delivery robot are shown in Figure 4.3.

4.2.2 Telepresence Function

Because of budget limitations many hospitals in developing countries cannot provide a viable Wi-Fi connection in all areas. Sometimes essential infrastructure is not present. So therefore a local network was selected as the first choice to compensate for this situation. A waterproof high-power outdoor Wi-Fi AP/Repeater, which has dual-band speeds of

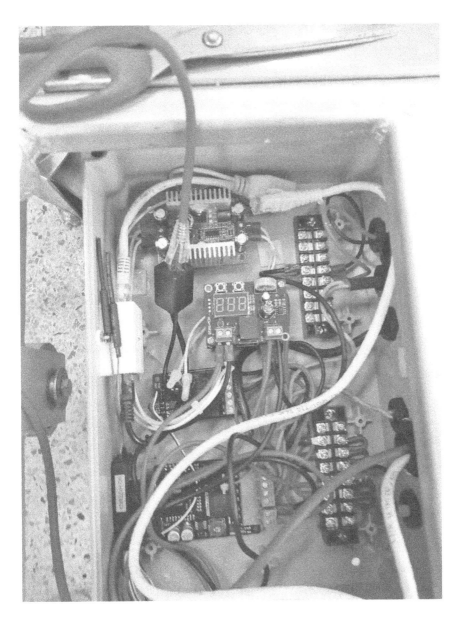

FIGURE 4.1　Electrical circuit of the driving system.

up to 2.4 GHz 150 Mbps and also 5 GHz 433 Mbps, was used to provide high performance communication for the telepresence system. A network camera, 5 MP IR fixed cube, lens 2.8 mm, was assembled with a Wi-Fi repeater. A local network from telepresence devices were joined

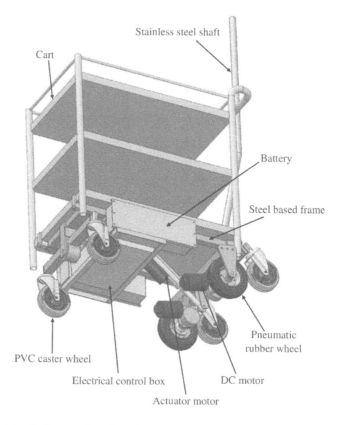

Stainless steel shaft

Cart

Battery

Steel based frame

Pneumatic
rubber wheel

PVC caster wheel

Electrical control box   DC motor

Actuator motor

FIGURE 4.2   Delivery robot drawing.

with a tablet PC, which was installed with iVMS-4200 client software for two-way communication.

4.3 RESULTS

The model of delivery and telepresence robot to help manage the ongoing COVID-19 crisis was fabricated and tested. The results are shown below:

4.3.1 Control Systems Test

The operative range, via the remote control, and the wireless camera, exceeded 50 m within a building and reached 100 m outdoors. Operators not familiar with this machine will need time to develop control skills because the robot caster wheels can be rotated in any direction. The prototype of this robot is shown in Figures 4.4 and 4.5. The test of Wi-Fi

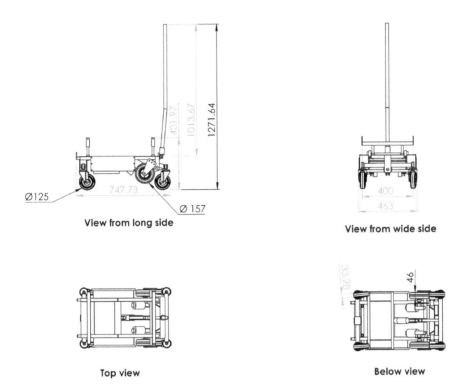

View from long side

View from wide side

Top view

Below view

FIGURE 4.3 Dimensions of the delivery robot (millimetre).

connection is shown in Figure 4.6. The test of delivery system is shown in Figures 4.7 and 4.8.

4.3.2 Driving and Loading Test

The actuator motor can lift the driving wheels up to 6 cm above the surface to prevent gear damage when the user needs to manually move the robot. The speed of the driving system is controlled at 1 m s^{-1} maximum speed. When operating on level ground, this robot, can carry up to 80 kg. The machine can cross a door sill or similar obstacle, measuring more than 3 cm in height. The robot can be amalgamated with a hospital cart easily by simply putting the cart on the top of the robot base frame. Because of the dual functions of the driving and steering systems, using the two-wheel drive, the robot needs only a little space for making a U-turn. When the user moves the remote-control button to let the robot run forward while turning left, then, the left wheel will slow down while the right wheel will be ongoing. If the machine operator orders the robot to turn right, without

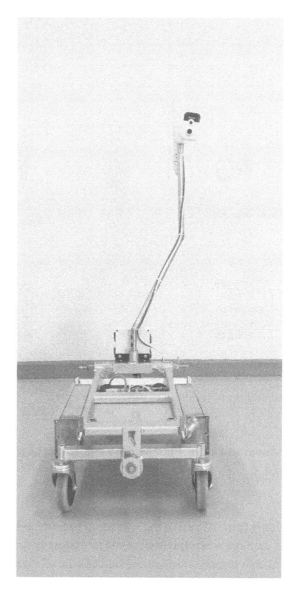

FIGURE 4.4 Delivery and telepresence robot (front view).

making a forward motion, the left wheel will turn steadily while the right wheel will be stationary.

4.3.3 Disinfectant Test

According to the concern about COVID-19 persists, the robot was tested with any disinfectant sprays and water. Results showed that cleaning agents as well as water cannot make contact with or damage the electrical

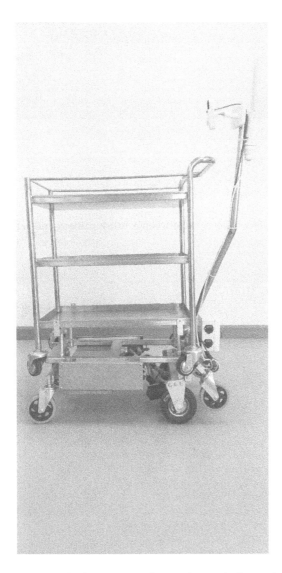

FIGURE 4.5 Delivery and telepresence robot with cart (side view).

devices which are located within the base frame. However, to prevent the long term electronics damage, rubbing the machine dry is recommended.

4.3.4 Cost-Effectiveness

The total cost of this machine that was calculated in Thai Baht (THB) is 111,500 THB. To discover the appropriate technique, some materials were bought with the uselessness of their applications. Therefore, to replicate this robot after the model is finalised, the budgets may decline approximately 30%.

FIGURE 4.6 Wi-Fi connection between a robot camera and a tablet PC within an emergency room.

FIGURE 4.7 The test of the delivery function when loaded to an 85 kg man.

FIGURE 4.8   The test of the driving system when operating on level ground, measuring 30°–45° in declination angle.

4.4 DISCUSSION

This delivery and telepresence robot was fabricated within the limitation of time as well as monetary resources. The machine has been used in the Mae Fah Luang University Medical Center Hospital, Chiang Rai Province, which is far away from Bangkok and also lacks raw materials. At this time, this robot is ready to support COVID-19 mitigation strategies, mostly limited to rooms within an inpatient faculty. However, now we have no COVID-19 case that has been detected within our healthcare service areas. Therefore, this machine has been used and tested in an emergency room. If we have time and budgets enough, for greater functionality, some technical details need to be addressed. On this version the telepresence system and delivery system are independent of each other so the user must control both devices simultaneously. A way to solve this problem would be to connect any robot control functions via a mobile application, which could provide robot control interaction using voice or touch screen in an all in one tablet. Because of incomplete obstacle detection and navigation systems, which were fabricated in a short time, the user must personally check for obstacles as the wireless camera has no obstacle detection function. A similar product in Turkey showed implementation of real time obstacle detection in a robotic cart using an android application, Arduino platform, which has a buzzer for proximity warning, a passive infrared sensor (PIR) to detect humans, an ultrasonic sensor to calculate the distances of objects or obstructions and also makes use of Bluetooth technology [8]. Ongoing research is in the development of autonomous navigating technology, which has been applied to a robotic vehicle for use in dangerous environments. This version has many functions, for example navigation, mapping and manipulation. The main structure of this autonomous robot also incorporates depth cameras, laser scanners, manipulators and also inertial measurement sensors [9]. These technologies may be merged with internet of things technology for the future versions.

Secondly, our present machine can be operated only either on the same floor or in open outdoor environs, although it could be moved to other floors using an elevator. For a genuine multi-floor transportation system, a mobile robot should be programmed with a multi-floor navigation system (e.g. mapping, path planning and localisation), elevator control system (3D camera and ultrasonic sensors), labware manipulation technology, which would be combined with an arm control system, and also a collision avoidance system [10, 11].

Finally, according to the axiomatic design (AD) theory, the trend of development of innovative medical devices requires a multi-functional conceptual design for delivering medical supplies. Therefore, the future healthcare delivery and telepresence robot should support varied delivery tasks, for example drugs, organs, fluids, surgical instruments, etc. Also a future medical robot should be developed that can control systems related to cooling, heating, humidifying and also dehumidifying, respectively [12].

4.5 CONCLUSIONS

This paper reveals the design and fabrication of a healthcare remote controlled transport robot, incorporating dual telepresence and delivery functions, to help mitigate the COVID-19 crisis. The functional concept required an optimum technology that can be available to low and middle-income countries. Medical personnel can assemble this machine easily by putting a cart onto the transport robot, the base frame of which can be adjusted according to the size of the cart. Waterproof and stainless-steel boxes can protect all machinery and electronic parts from corrosive agents, which would be used for robot cleaning. The present telecommunication system is suitable for use in both indoor and outdoor environments. According to the trial results, future research should consider development of the delivery control system becoming amalgamated with the telepresence system via internet of things technology. The navigation system being able to detect obstacles and then linking to a mapping recognition software. The manipulator technology being able to support multi-floor transportation via an elevator, and finally a multi-functional robot being able to assist with some medical tasks.

4.6 ACKNOWLEDGEMENTS

The inventor would like to thank Dr. Roger Timothy Callaghan, School of Medicine, Mae Fah Luang University for linguistic analysis, Watchara Jamnuch as well as Thanat Sirsuksan, an electrical engineer, for technical information.

DECLARATIONS

Funding: The funding support was provided by the Princess Srinagarindra's Centenary Celebrations Foundation, Mae Fah Luang University, fiscal year 2020, Memorandum No. 28/2563.

Conflicts of interest/Competing interests: The author has no conflict of interest to declare.

Availability of data and material: Not applicable.

Code availability: Not applicable.

Authors' contributions: Arnon Jumlongkul created this robot as well as drafted the manuscript solely.

Ethics approval: Not applicable.

Consent to participate: Not applicable.

Consent for publication: I, the undersigned, give my **consent** for the **publication** of identifiable details, which can include photograph(s) and/or videos and/or case history and/or details within the text ('Material') to be published in the above Journal and Article.

REFERENCES

1. Centers for Disease Control and Prevention. Social Distancing [Internet]. 2020 [cited 2020 May 18]. Available from: https://www.cdc.gov/coronavirus/2019-ncov/prevent-getting-sick/social-distancing.html
2. Cresswell K, Cunningham-Burley S, Sheikh A. Health Care Robotics: Qualitative Exploration of Key Challenges and Future Directions. J Med Internet Res. 2018 04;20(7):e10410.
3. Acosta Calderon CA, Mohan ER, Ng BS. Development of a hospital mobile platform for logistics tasks. Digit Commun Netw. 2015 Apr;1(2):102–11.
4. Kristoffersson A, Coradeschi S, Loutfi A. A Review of Mobile Robotic Telepresence. Adv Hum-Comput Interact. 2013;2013:1–17.
5. Tavakoli M, Carriere J, Torabi A. Robotics, Smart Wearable Technologies, and Autonomous Intelligent Systems for Healthcare During the COVID-19 Pandemic: An Analysis of the State of the Art and Future Vision. Adv Intell Syst. 2020 May 5;2000071.
6. Khan ZH, Siddique A, Lee CW. Robotics Utilization for Healthcare Digitization in Global COVID-19 Management. Int J Environ Res Public Health. 2020 May 28;17(11):3819.
7. Zeng Z, Chen P-J, Lew AA. From High-touch to high-tech: COVID-19 Drives Robotics Adoption. Tour Geogr. 2020 May 26;22(3):724–34.
8. Yılmaz E, Özyer ST. Remote and Autonomous Controlled Robotic Car based on Arduino with Real Time Obstacle Detection and Avoidance. Univers J Eng Sci. 2019 Jan;7(1):1–7.
9. Losch R, Grehl S, Donner M, Buhl C, Jung B. Design of an Autonomous Robot for Mapping, Navigation, and Manipulation in Underground Mines. In: 2018 IEEE/RSJ International Conference on Intelligent Robots and Systems (IROS) [Internet]. Madrid: IEEE; 2018 [cited 2020 Jul 10]. p. 1407–12. Available from: https://ieeexplore.ieee.org/document/8594190/
10. Thurow K, Zhang L, Liu H, Junginger S, Stoll N, Huang J. Multi-floor Laboratory Transportation Technologies Based on Intelligent Mobile Robots. Transp Saf Environ. 2019 Jul 1;1(1):37–53.
11. Abdulla AA, Liu H, Stoll N, Thurow K. A New Robust Method for Mobile Robot Multifloor Navigation in Distributed Life Science Laboratories. J Control Sci Eng. 2016;2016:1–17.
12. Zhu A, Zou C, Luo W, He R. The Demand-driven Conceptual Design of Multi-function Modular Cabinet for Medical Delivery Robot. Procedia CIRP. 2016;53:273–7.

CHAPTER 5

Concept of an Autonomous Robot for Medical Services, Rehabilitation and Music Therapy for Pandemics

Sergey V. Shushardzhan

The Scientific Research Center for Music Therapy and Healthcare Technologies LLC, Moscow, Russia

CONTENTS

DOI: 10.1201/9781003195061-5

5.1 INTRODUCTION

The pandemic outbreak of coronavirus disease in 2019 and its rapid spread around the World led to the infection of more than 160 million people on the planet and the death of over 3 million people. It became the reason that COVID-19 was included in a number of the most current problems of our time.

It is obvious that mass immunisation of the population, on which justified hopes are pinned, is not enough for complete control over the COVID-19 pandemic because due to the economic and technical problems it is extremely uneven in different regions of the world. In this regard, in general, the spread rate of infection is still ahead of the vaccination rate. The catastrophic events in India, the exploding site of infection in other countries confirm it.

Some systemic problems of medical and tactical nature that require an obligatory solution are also disclosed in the process of the analysis of current events.

That is why we decided to discuss the following topical issues in this chapter:

1. What were the main challenges for the healthcare system concerning the COVID-19 pandemic?

2. What new opportunities in the rehabilitation treatment of patients with COVID-19 do open scientific music therapy (SMT) and its technologies integrated into artificial intelligence software?

3. How can medical robotics play one of the most important roles in the struggle with coronavirus infection and its consequences?

4. Finally, a conceptual model of an autonomous multifunctional robot for medical services, rehabilitation and music therapy will be represented here as a practical step to an innovative response to the complex challenges concerning the COVID-19 pandemic.

5.2 MEDICAL, SOCIAL AND PSYCHOLOGICAL IMPACT OF PANDEMIC

5.2.1 Epidemiology

According to the Web portal 'Coronavirus Today' on the 13 May 2021, 160,525,159 people were infected with coronavirus in the world, the death toll is 3,333,729 [1], and 1,313,443,562 people were vaccinated.

The vaccination rate in the world is uneven; it depends on the economic condition, population, geographic location and organisational conformity of the Government in each particular country.

Scientists from all over the world concur in the opinion that 75% of the world's population must be vaccinated to form herd immunity from COVID.

According to the Bloomberg agency, for example for Israel, only two months are needed at the current vaccination rate to vaccinate 75% of the country's population from coronavirus as it will take nine months to vaccinate the same percentage of the population in the US, and seven months in the UK. Canada will spend the most time on vaccination at the current rate; it needs about ten years, while the vaccination of 75% of the world's population will take about seven years [2].

If it continues in such a way and keeping in mind any possible virus mutations and the threat of the new site of infection in low developed countries, it is not difficult to predict the protracted nature of pandemic response with new millions of deaths among the world's population and the global economic problems.

That is the way to eliminate the pandemic in the nearest future and increase the rate of vaccination, it is necessary to enhance the effectiveness of the entire complex of anti-epidemic measures.

Nonetheless, it is extremely important to prevent nosocomial infection and prevent the activation of the site of infection in medical organisations [3]. And here medical robotics has huge untapped opportunities. In the relevant section of this chapter, we will provide a rationale for this thesis.

5.2.2 Clinical Aspects of Coronavirus Infection

It is known that the coronavirus infection COVID-19 (Corona Virus Disease 2019, WHO, 02/11/2020) is an acute respiratory disease caused by the new coronavirus (SARS-CoV-2), associated with increased mortality among people over the age of 60 and also the persons with comorbid pathological conditions such as cardiovascular diseases, chronic respiratory diseases, diabetes and cancer [3].

It was found that COVID-19 can occur both in asymptomatic and mild clinical forms (80%) and in severe clinical forms (20%) with the development of community-acquired pneumonia, respiratory distress syndrome and respiratory failure. It is known that coronavirus infection can attack the nervous system, gastrointestinal tract and other vital organs, but the most common clinical form is bilateral pneumonia [4].

According to the literature data, including Chinese authors who have perhaps the most significant experience, the main goal of rehabilitation in patients with COVID-19 is, first of all, the restoration of the respiratory system and respiratory function and the removal of anxiety-depressive states, restoration of disordered functions and improving the life quality [5].

5.2.3 COVID-19 and Mental Disorders

More recently, another serious problem of the pandemic has appeared, and it is mental disorders.

- They are regularly observed in patients with moderate and severe forms of this illness who feel physically suffering from pulmonary insufficiency and numerous complications. Such conditions almost always go along with the increased anxiety and fears.

- However, it is found out that not less than 60% of patients who have come through COVID-19 successfully, subsequently these patients also suffer from serious mental disorders, including depression, anxiety, insomnia, etc.

- Finally, according to the diverse sources, a part of the population (4–10% according to the different authors), who is on self-isolation, takes restrictions with difficulty, as a result, they feel stress and suffer from anxiety-depressive disorders.

It was found out that long-lived neuroticisms not only reduce the quality of life and seriously complicate current diseases but can also cause new sufferings such as serious psychosomatic disorders and even cancer.

5.2.4 Social Impact of Pandemic

We should not forget that during a pandemic, not only infected patients suffer. Hundreds of millions of people, due to quarantine measures, were involved in a stressful situation caused by fears, forced isolation and economic problems.

The public health authorities were in a quandary for a time and acted not very effectively. Then the attention was focused on the development of vaccines, which is understandable. But, unfortunately, hardly anybody thought about the psychological support of huge masses of people who were in a stressful state staying-at-home, many of whom lost their business/work and their usual way of life and interpersonal communication.

And this situation is naturally in evidence. We saw two scenarios of the development of the events.

The first scenario. There are numerous protests around the world against quarantine measures and restrictions. As the video shows, many people often behaved aggressively, emotionally and inappropriately. People have stopped neither common sense nor the risk of infection, they were in a state of unresolved stress and emotion.

The second scenario. A certain part of people who were in self-isolation, intuitively take interest in music and art. Let us remind the footage that went around the world when the Italians went out the balconies of their houses and played music and sang together. It helped to raise their spirits, not to give up in the face of a pandemic and safely go through the hardship. Today, such concerts have become common practice in many countries, demonstrating the health-improving potential of creativity.

The world community must make serious conclusions from the current events.

One of them is that people who are under stress during a pandemic are at risk. Continued mental stress negatively affects human health, reduces immunity and thus there is incidence.

Considering that today almost hundreds of millions of the world's populations are included in this problem it becomes clear that, to reduce the incidence, it is necessary to improve the system of not only epidemiological but also global psychological assistance to the population. Here we cannot be without creating powerful Internet portals integrated with artificial intelligence and telemedicine capabilities.

In that case, SMT, which has a rather wide range of methods and advanced technologies, can play an important role in providing mass psychological support and medical rehabilitation at all stages of patients with COVID-19 [6–8].

5.3 CONCERNING SCIENTIFIC MUSIC THERAPY AND PROSPECTS OF ITS USE IN THE REHABILITATION OF PATIENTS WITH COVID-19

5.3.1 From the History of Music Therapy

Therapeutic use of music has a long history. Hippocrates, Aristotle and others ancient sages a thousand years ago were trying to treat with music nervous and mental patients. There are a lot of documentary mentions. They refer to different periods and civilisations and give a clear idea that music in medicine has been used, but empirically, the explanations of therapeutic effects were based on myths, metaphysical theories, or religious views.

In the 20th century, music therapy has been widely practiced in various European countries and the United States. National Music Therapy Associations were established in England, Germany, Holland, France, Belgium, Italy, etc. Music therapy was recognised in the United States after the Second World War when music was successfully applied in the treatment of emotional disorders among war veterans. Currently, there are around 3500 professional music therapists registered in the United States, and the need for specialists that profile has been steadily increasing. More than 100 universities and colleges all over the world offer educational programs, after which students receive a Bachelor's degree, Master's, or Doctoral degree in this field.

5.3.2 Features of Scientific Music Therapy

SMT is the new interdisciplinary direction of music therapy based on the synthesis of Medicine, Physics, Arts and Modern Technologies. Fundamentals of SMT were developed in Russia - by the efforts of the author of this article in the early nineties of the last century. In Russia, various researches of SMT are concentrated in the Scientific Research Center for Music Therapy and Healthcare Technologies (SRC MT HT) in Moscow which has close cooperation with teams of specialists from different countries.

In 2019 year, SMT received the new international confirmation of its importance. The European Union has issued a special grant to an international group of specialists from Russia, Slovakia, Great Britain, Estonia and the Czech Republic: 'Comprehensive multi-professional approach to the treatment the patients using the elements of the scientific music therapy'. That international group has been working in cooperation with the aforementioned SRC MT HT for several years, in particular, based on Russian technologies, 11 Russian patents and some know-how (see, for example patents [9–17].

In clinical studies of SRC MT HT, various therapeutic and health effects of music therapy have been identified: neurohumoral, psychotherapeutic, analgesic, adaptogenic, regenerative, hypotensive, etc. [18–22].

Thanks to the multi-method research of music's influence on the body several innovative technologies have been developed. Today there are more than 50 methods.

There are receptive methods of music therapy, where the patient passively receives the procedure, and active ones, where the patient himself takes part in it directly, for example singing or learning to play the elementary musical instruments. High-tech methods are marked separately which use digital technologies and artificial intelligence [23].

5.3.3 Musical-Acoustic Algorithms as a Tool for Regulation of Vital Functions and Psychotherapy

SMT has a preference to study the features of complex body reactions – psychological, physiological and bio-physical – to music by various modern diagnostic technologies.

In the course of these researches, three main musical-acoustic algorithms were discovered (S – sedative, T – tonic and HR – harmonising), which differ from each other in frequency, amplitude, the intensity of sound impact, certain musical characteristics.

In experiments (1996–2020) it was shown, that *different algorithms of direct musical - acoustic impacts significantly change the vital activity of cells cultured in Vitro*: in some cases, activate, in others, inhibit [23].

Moreover, each algorithm cause characteristic changes in the state of the nervous system and the level of hormones in the blood.

Some following regularities were experimentally revealed:

1. S-algorithms inhibit the activity of the cerebral cortex and stimulate the activity of the parasympathetic nervous system, which causes

mental and muscle relaxation, slows down the heart rate and lowers blood pressure. S-algorithms reduce an elevated blood level of adrenaline, noradrenaline and cortisol.

2. T-algorithms act in exactly the opposite way.

3. HR algorithms bring the nervous and hormonal systems into a state of equilibrium and stability, which has a positive influence on the body, including the anti-aging effect.

Using found algorithms in digital music therapy programs is the key to psychotherapy and hormonal level optimising, which is important for organism regulation and health improvement.

The results of our long-time scientific research and the world experience of music therapy were generalised in the form of a Neurohormonal-Resonance Theory of Acoustical Influences, which was proposed in 2005 (S. Shushardzhan), became theoretical basement of SMT and gained international recognition.

Scientific Music Therapists have a clear idea of the algorithmic mechanisms of music influence on a person, knows how to carry out the necessary diagnostics and choose the best method or technology needed in each specific case. SMT provides more qualified help and significantly higher efficacy in treatment compared to intuitive-empirical approaches.

5.3.4 Methods of Music Therapy, Digital Technologies and Software in the Rehabilitation of Patients with COVID-19

Receptive, active and high-tech methods can be used in the rehabilitation process the choice of which will be depended on the specific tasks.

Special precedence is given to digital music therapy programs and modern telemedicine technologies, which allow taking online medical individual and group sessions for people who need the treatment and psychological support.

It is determined that COVID-19 has a marked neurotropicity [24]. At the same time, anxiety-depressive states are a common syndrome in patients with COVID-19, the quality of life is significantly reducing, all it urgently requires psychotherapeutic treatment in the complex of rehabilitation measures.

In this sense, the music, which the great Russian neurologist Bekhterev called '… the sovereign of thoughts and feelings', is one of the favourites. The influence of music on the emotional sphere has been obvious to great doctors since ancient times, and they used it for psychotherapeutic purposes.

Let's consider some of the methods and technologies of music therapy shown to work in the rehabilitation of patients with COVID-19.

5.3.4.1 Digital Music Psychotherapy

We have developed some digital computer programs based on regulator algorithms that are used for stress, neurosis, insomnia, psychosomatic disorders and life quality decrease in the condition of the monotonous atmosphere. The sessions of music psychotherapy are held in specially equipped patient rooms where the patients are listening to treatment programs for 20–30 minutes. Any computer system with speakers or headphones is enough for it.

The doctors of any specialties, nurses, psychologists, etc. even without special training can successfully use music therapy in treatment, prophylactic and rehabilitation work and they also can do it Online.

5.3.4.2 Virtual Music-Art Therapy (VMARTT)

This is an innovative method of psychotherapy and personality development in the form of separate audio-visual digital computer programs where the world's masterpieces of painting and musical art are used.

Remarkable landscapes, forests and fields, high seas, medieval castles and bright characters, sunsets and sunrises, seasons, all these picturesque creations as if come to life against the background of brilliant music.

Clinical researches in different age groups have shown that if to use VMARTT for people who suffer from emotional lability and increased anxiety, in 84% of the cases the neurotic symptoms fade away and the emotional state stabilizes, which was objectively confirmed by psychodiagnostic tests of Luscher, Taylor, and example, 88% of the patients of the main group noticed the aesthetic pleasure of watching virtual music-art therapy programs and an increased interest to musical art and painting.

Thanks to digital performance, effective and easy-to-use virtual music art therapy programs can be transmitted online to smartphones, personal computers and televisions. This is very important to use in COVID-19 hospitals and rehabilitation centres.

5.3.4.3 Vocal Therapy

Taking into consideration that the main target organ of the coronavirus is the lungs, it is recommended to use various types of breathing exercises in the rehabilitation of the patients.

At the same time, there is a well-known medical and health-improving method called in 1993 by the author, Shushardzhan S.V. 'the vocal therapy' which is based on the principles of classical singing and a special voice training system which is aimed at developing and strengthening of the respiratory system, vibration-acoustic stimulation of the activity of the vital organs, the optimisation of higher nervous activity and increasing of the body defences.

The medical and health effects of vocal therapy in the best way possible are suited for solving many actual problems of the recovery period of patients with COVID-19, especially in the category of patients '60+', who are at risk.

It was found out that the systemic use of vocal therapy causes marked positive dynamics of indicators of lung capacity, and also positively gets into the psycho-emotional state and the memory of patients [18].

It makes sense to take vocal therapy sessions in hospitals and rehabilitation centres for the patients with COVID-19 in the telemedicine option, which reduces the risk of the spread of nosocomial infection and saves the medical staff energy.

Hereafter we will discuss the special opportunities that appear when integrating digital music therapy technologies into the artificial intelligence of medical robots.

5.4 THE ROLE OF MEDICAL ROBOTICS IN MODERN HEALTHCARE AND THE LIQUIDATION OF THE PANDEMIC CONSEQUENCES

In the 21st century, robotics has entered almost all spheres of activity of our civilisation. Medical robotics has made a particularly rapid leap over the past two decades which has a wide range of varieties.

For instance, surgical robots which are remotely controlled help doctors to perform highly accurate and minimally invasive operations.

There are also robotic assistants which deliver drugs and food to patients and staff; rehabilitation robots; robots-disinfectors; robot-companion or empathic robots which assist in the elderly care or patients with physical/mental disabilities; robots for psychotherapy.

Finally, nanorobots which are equal to molecules are designed to carry out certain programs inside their bodies and they can move, take, analyse and transmit different information.

Medical robotics is now used in almost all areas of healthcare in developed countries.

According to the conviction of experts from the United States of America, the use of robotics in health care can provide high-intensity therapy [25].

5.4.1 Main Types of Rehabilitation Robotics

Rehabilitation robots which are divided into assistants and therapeutic robotic systems play an important role in restoring physical activity and improving the quality of handicapped people's life.

Assistant robots are meant to help people with reduced capabilities in solving urgent everyday tasks, which cannot do their job due to their health condition, for example some social and domestic actions. Robots can bring some food to the mouth of a disabled person or turn over pages in a book. In this case, stationary robots are fixed in a certain position on workstations and are controlled by typed commands through various devices. Mobile robots on the other hand typically consist of a movable arm fixed either on a mobile platform or the lateral side of a motorised wheelchair. [26].

Rehabilitation robotics for therapeutic purposes includes various types of programmable stationary or portable electromechanical devices and fitness equipment, the main purpose of which is to recover the disordered function of organism in the first instance motor inducted by neurological disorders or trauma [27].

The motor function recovery among patients with cerebral spinal injury, despite the development of modern medicine, remains a serious problem. Recovery level after spinal cord trauma is often small and many patients stay wheelchair-bound. As a result of low physical activity, secondary affection gradually develops among victims (osteoporosis, obesity, cardiovascular, respiratory, genitourinary, trophic and other disorders), the confounding flowing of the basic disease and the complicating process of medical rehabilitation [28].

Improvement of functional mobility and general health condition can be achieved with the use of robotic devices [29]. It is expected that the growth of robotic devices focused on specific rehabilitation therapy for a patient at home [30].

Reasonable hopes are tied to the use of exoskeletons and computer-aided systems of movement.

Exoskeletons are wireframe devices that are fixed outside of the human body and are meant for the improvement of lost/reduced motor functions, increasing muscle strength and range of movement.

There are active models of exoskeletons that use external devices as a source of energy and are used in rehabilitation, whereas the passive exoskeletons which have mainly military use are based on the use of kinetic energy and human strength. Besides, there are also exoskeletons of the upper/lower limbs and exoskeletons suits [31].

Positive results of the rehabilitation of patients with the consequences of spinal cord injury were got through a mix of the exoskeleton using the functional electrical stimulation of the lower limbs. When compared with the control group that received the traditional rehabilitation complex, the electromyography parameters of the back muscles and hip joint extensors, the biomechanical parameters of walking and the psychological status scale in the main group looked more preferable. At the same time, the walking of the patients of the main group became more stable and less energy-consuming. Training with the use of an exoskeleton ameliorated a significant improvement in the psychological status, and in general, expanded the functions of self-care and mobility among patients of the main group [32].

Robotic systems for movement are designed to optimise the repetitive training required for improving motor function among patients with disorders tied to neurological diseases [9].

Under the circumstances, early intensive and long-term rehabilitation of advanced robotic devices are critical factors for achieving good results [33].

The intensity of rehabilitation leads to staff costs increasing and the time limitation for hospital staying is a restriction. In this scenario, robotics can make it possible to increase the effectiveness of physical activity rehabilitation [34].

A meta-analysis has shown that arm training with robotics improves the quality of daily life and also the motor activity of the upper limbs [35].

The modern world almost wholly depends on advanced technology, therefore elaboration of robotics, software, computer control systems, including a Brain–Computer Interface that provides a communication path between the human brain and the computer system for Physically Handicapped People is the prospective direction of development [36–38].

5.4.2 New Tasks of Rehabilitation Robots in a Pandemic Time

The COVID-19 pandemic has had a huge impact on all spheres of modern life of the world's population and has identified new challenges facing the global health system, including medical service and rehabilitation.

An increasing flow of patients with respiratory, psychosomatic and stress-related disorders after the coronavirus infection has joined the usual contingent of rehabilitation centres. Treatment-and-prophylactic institutions work with great overload, there is not enough medical staff.

At the same time, the risk of repeated outbreaks of coronavirus and other types of dangerous infections remains. Among the identified foci of reinfection medical and social institutions are in the first positions.

To enhance the effectiveness of remediation of a pandemic in rehabilitation centres and hospitals, it is necessary to define the main challenges for the time-critical issue.

So, if we sum up the results of our analysis, then these challenges include:

- *The risk of the spread of coronavirus and the other types of infection in health care institutions*

- *An increasing number of patients with stressful and psychosomatic disorders*

- *An increasing number of patients with adverse respiratory effects after suffering from coronavirus pneumonia*

- *Psychophysical overload of the medical staff*

The institutions of different countries are engaged in the search for antiviral drugs and vaccines, and there has been some progress in this direction. However, the abovementioned pandemic challenges will remain relevant for a long time.

It should be understood that for many disabled patients who undergo rehabilitation treatment in rehabilitation centres, for example with movement disorders after strokes or traumatic brain injuries, a coronavirus infection or another type of infection can be fatal.

Besides, the epidemiological, pharmaceutical and biotechnological efforts undertaken by the health care system as a whole, several complex measures are needed in medical institutions to maximise the effective response to the challenges in a pandemic:

- *Regular disinfection of all rooms and public places*

- *Minimising contact of medical staff with quarantined persons*

- *Introduction of programs for early rehabilitation of respiratory disorders after suffering from coronavirus pneumonia*

- *Widespread use of psychotherapy and psycho correction methods in rehabilitation programs for patients of any profile, including patients with stressful and psychosomatic disorders after COVID-19*

The implementation of these tasks is a huge additional burden both for the budget of medical institutions and for the staff, the shortage of which has recently been very noticeable.

In a pandemic, the intensive connection of robotics and IT technologies is critically necessary to the work of rehabilitation centres and other medical institutions. In this case, new generation robotics is needed with a set of functions capable to solve holistically the most pressing challenge.

5.4.3 The Autonomous Multifunctional Medical Robot 'Helper'

In 2019 together with partners from the «Time of Robots» LLC we created an autonomous medical robot based on the R. Bot 100 Plus platform, known for its large work resource and high reliability. A pilot sample could move along the specified routes, communicate, carry out biometric identification and select health-improving music tracks [39].

Currently, to the basic capabilities of the robot, called 'Helper' we have added four functions that are critical in the face of a pandemic:

- *Disinfection of premises and robot self-disinfection*

- *Drugs delivery*

- *Telemedicine*

- *Interactive music therapy and virtual music-art therapy*

The Helper robot has a male and female speech synthesiser, the ability to connect to interactive services, and can work both autonomously and under the control of a remote user/operator.

With a height of 105 cm robot weighs 45 kg, is capable of operating from a rechargeable battery for up to 12 hours, self-charging up to 5 hours. The technical features are shown in Figure 5.1.

5.4.3.1 Disinfection of Premises and Self-Disinfection

The 'Helper' robot is capable of automatically performing complex disinfection of premises up to 150 sq.m. medical offices, wards, halls and corridors, public places. This gadget is capable of identifying a person and also switching over to a safe for people mode of disinfection.

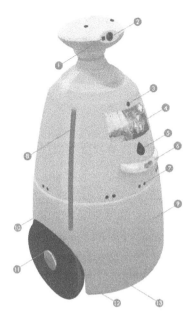

Technical features:

1. Temperature sensor.
2. Main camera
3. Camera for autonomous movement.
4. Touch screen
5. Medication control camera.
6. Drug delivery cassette.
7. Ultrasonic obstacle sensors.
8. External germicidal lamps.
9. Driving wheels.
10. Bactericidal recirculator.
11. Bactericidal floor lamp.
12. Acoustic speakers.

Additional options

❖ Distance range up to 300 metres
❖ 2 wireless connections (Wi-Fi 4G)
❖ Battery life up to 16 hours

FIGURE 5.1 Technical features of the multifunctional autonomous robot 'Helper'.

External germicidal or UV lamps (Figure 5.1, number 8) are used as equipment for disinfection of empty rooms and a built-in air recirculator with filtration and radiation disinfection (10), a bactericidal lamp for the floor is used as equipment for disinfection of rooms with human presence (11).

5.4.3.2 Personalised Medicines Delivery

Under the conditions of increased epidemiological danger, medicine delivery and medical consumables (if necessary) give the possibility to prevent infection of medical staff and patients. The technical support is carried out by using a multi-section self-retractable cassette (6), which is pre-filled with medicine by medical prescription. The self-disinfection option excludes the possibility of contact infection of transported medicines, and the biometric identification function of people allows controlling medicine delivery.

5.4.3.3 Telemedicine

With the help of the main telepresence camera (2) and the robot, it is possible to conduct various remote training and rehabilitation programs.

So, for example for the correction of respiratory disorders among patients after coronavirus pneumonia, the use of vocal therapy is needed as an effective method of rehabilitation treatment through singing.

Also, the patients who are quarantined can use early intensive rehabilitation participating in online training such as breathing exercises, physiotherapy complexes, etc.

At the same time, two-way remote communication eliminates the risk of mutual infection of patients and medical staff.

5.4.3.4 Interactive Music Therapy and Virtual Music-Art Therapy

The coronavirus pandemic has found out a serious problem such as various stress disorders and panic attacks, which became widespread among patients and the population of the planet.

Based on the advanced achievements of scientific music therapy, bio-acoustics and psychology, innovative programs for psycho diagnostics and music-acoustic psychotherapy in digital format have been developed. The corresponding software is included in the robot's functionality. Thanks to these programs, the robot asks questions, analyses the answers received and, on their basis, accurately selects therapeutic music tracks suitable for a particular patient.

It has been found that their use is an effective way to relieve stress and various psychosomatic disorders [39]. Two acoustic speakers, 20 W each (12), transmit high-quality sound.

A 7-inch touch screen existence (4) allows carrying out the robot another innovative method such as virtual music-art therapy where the world masterpieces of musical art and painting are used. The capabilities of Wi-Fi and Bluetooth technologies allow the robot, if necessary, to broadcast treatment programs on the screens of personal computers and TVs.

At the same time, these methods of psychological relief can be used both in working with patients and with medical staff.

5.5 CONCLUSION

Medical robotics must play an increasingly important role in the process of modern rehabilitation treatment and hospital services, which become especially great during a pandemic control and liquidation of its consequences.

What can be expected in the case of systematic implementation of autonomous multifunctional robots of our concept in medical and rehabilitation practice?

- Significant reduction in nosocomial infection

- Improvement of the epidemiological situation

- Reducing workload on medical staff

- Expanding the range of medical rehabilitation services provided

- Improving the psychological state of patients and quality of life

- Increasing the intensification and efficiency of the work of a medical institution

Thanks to the combination of several functions, autonomous multifunctional robots like 'Helper' will also be useful for medical institutions of any profile, not only in pandemic time but also in everyday practice.

We believe that the integration of science, technology and art is the future of artificial intelligence and robotics. The use of music and other types of art in the functionality of robots brings them closer to humans. Such an innovative approach opens up new opportunities in medical service and communication.

The global robotisation of the healthcare system has strategic importance with high medical, social and economic potential.

REFERENCES

1. Coronavirus today URL: https://koronavirustoday.ru/info/koronavirus-tablicza-po-stranam-mira-na-segodnya/

2. Bloomberg Agency URL: https://www.bloomberg.com/graphics/covid-vaccine-tracker-globaldistribution/?sref =Y0jVLcFo

3. 'Epidemiology and Prevention of COVID-19'. Guidelines MP 3.1.0170-20 (in edition MP 3.1.0175-20 'Changes № 1 in MP 3.1.0170-20 "Epidemiology and Prevention of COVID-19", approved by Federal Service for Surveillance on Consumer Rights Protection and Human Welfare 30.04.2020')

4. Temporary guidelines 'Prevention, diagnosis, and treatment of new coronavirus infection' (COVID-19). Version 6 (28.04.2020)" (approved by Ministry of Health of Russia). P. 1–18. URL: https://static1.rosminzdrav.ru/system/attachments/attaches/000/050/122/original/28042020 _%D0%9CR_COVID-19_v6.pdf

5. Wang T.J., Chau B., Lui M., Lam G.T., Lin N., Humbert S. Physical medicine and rehabilitation and pulmonary rehabilitation for COVID-19. American Journal of Physical Medicine & Rehabilitation. 2020 Sep; 99(9):769–774. DOI: 10.1097/PHM.0000000000001505. PMID: 32541352

6. Burkhart Chr. Music therapy providing some calm during COVID-19 Published: Aug. 27, 2020, at 3:41 PM GMT+3. URL: https://www.abc12.com/2020/08/27/music-therapy-providing-some-calm-during-covid-19/

7. Giordano F., Scarlata E., Baroni M., Gentile E., Puntillo F., Brienza N., Gesualdo L. Receptive music therapy to reduce stress and improve wellbeing in Italian clinical staff involved in COVID-19 pandemic: A preliminary

study. The Arts in Psychotherapy. 2020, 70, September 2020, 101688/ Received 16 June 2020, Revised 8 July 2020, Accepted 11 July 2020, Available online 15 July 2020. URL: https://doi.org/10.1016/j.aip. 2020. 101688

8. Mastnak W. Psychopathological problems related to the COVID-19 pandemic and possible prevention with music therapy. First published: 12 May 2020. URL: https://doi.org/10.1111/apa.15346

9. Shushardzhan S.V. The method of changing the activity of microorganisms in vitro. Patent No. 2195493. Russian Patent and Trademark Agency (2002).

10. Shushardzhan S.V. The method for potentiating the therapeutic effect by a combination of musical-acoustic and medicinal effects. Patent No. 22240146. The Federal Service for Intellectual Property, Patents, and Trademarks (2004).

11. Shushardzhan S.V. The method for correcting the state of coagulation of human blood. Patent No. 2336098. The Federal Service for Intellectual Property, Patents, and Trademarks (2008).

12. Shushardzhan S.V. The method of healing and rejuvenation of the skin. Patent number 2429026. Registered in the Russian State Register of Inventions (2011).

13. Shushardzhan, S.V. Software and acoustic complex Profi-Grand. Patent number 126602. Registered in the State Register of Inventions of the Russian Federation (2013).

14. Shushardzhan S.V., Shushardzhan R.S. Device for musical acoustic magnetic-vacuum effects on acupuncture points and reflexogenic zones Akuton. Patent number 129398. Registered in the State Register of Inventions of the Russian Federation (2013).

15. Shushardzhan S.V. Device for skin rejuvenation and recovery Bonnie Grand. Patent number 129820. Registered in the Russian State Register of Inventions (2013).

16. Shushardzhan S.V. The method of enhancing the growth of leukocyte mass and the complex correction of the blood in Vitro. Patent number 2518534. Registered in the State Register of Inventions of the Russian Federation (2014).

17. Shushardzhan S.V. The method of neuro-hormonal correction and rejuvenation with the help of musical-acoustic effects. Patent No. 2518538. Registered in the State Register of Inventions of the Russian Federation (2014).

18. Shushardzhan S.V. Music therapy guidance. Medicine. 2005. P.-478

19. Shushardzhan S.V., Shushardzhan R.S., Eremina N.I. Substantiation of the reflex-resonance theory of acoustic influences and the prospects for the use of music therapy technologies. Bulletin of Rehabilitation Medicine. 3 (31). 2009. P. 34–37

20. do Amaral M.A.S., Neto M.G., de Queiroz J.G., Martins-Filho P.R.S., Saquetto M.B., Oliveira Carvalho V.C. Effect of music therapy on blood pressure of individuals with hypertension: A systematic review and meta-analysis. International Journal of Cardiology. 2016 Jul 1; 214: 461–4. DOI: 10.1016/P.-197.

21. Mitrovic, P., Stefanovic, B., Paladin, A., Radovanovic, M., Radovanovic, N., Rajic, D., Matic, G., Novakovic, A., Mijic, N., Vasiljevic, Z. The Music Therapy in hypertensive patients with acute myocardial infarction after previous coronary artery bypass surgery. Journal of Hypertension. 2015 June; Volume 33, P. -134

22. Zanini, C., Sousa, A.L., Teixeira, D., Jardim, P.C., Pereira, D. Vilela, B. Music therapy as part of the treatment of hypertensive patients. Journal of Hypertension. 2018 June; Volume 36, P. -260

23. Shushardzhan, S. Scientific Music Therapy - achievements and prospects. Slovakia, Šamorin, Proceedings of the XXI Interdisciplinary Medical Congress of Natural Medicine with International Participation. 2017. P.- 17

24. Baig, A.M., Khaleeq, A., Ali, U., Syeda, H. Evidence of the COVID-19 virus targeting the CNS: tissue distribution, host-virus interaction, and proposed neurotropic mechanisms. ACS Chemical Neuroscience. 2020; 11(7):995–998. URL: https://doi.org/10.1021/ acschemneuro. 0c00122.

25. Scott, S.H., Dukelow, S.P.. Potential of robots as next-generation technology for clinical assessment of neurological disorders and upper-limb therapy. Journal of Rehabilitation Research and Development. 2011; 48(4), 335–354. doi:10.1682/JRRD.2010. 04.0057

26. Gill, C. Robotics in the Rehabilitation of Neurological Conditions. George Washington University. 2015. URL: https://www.researchgate.net/publication/ 278243800

27. Thierry, K. Rehabilitation Robotics: What are the benefits? Open Access Government, 2015. URL: https://www.openaccessgovernment.org/

28. Karyakin, N.N., Belova, A.N., Sushin, V.O., Sheiko, G.E., Israelian, Y.A., Litvinova, N.Y. Potential advantages and limitations of the use of robotic exoskeletons in patients with spinal cord injury: state of the question. Bulletin of Rehabilitation Medicine. 2020; 2:68–78. DOI: 10.38025/ 2078-1962-2020-96-2-68-78

29. Tefertiller, C., Pharo, B., Evans, N., Winchester, P. Efficacy of rehabilitation robotics for walking training in neurological disorders: A review. Journal of Rehabilitation Research and Development. 2011; 48(4):387–416. DOI: 10.1682/JRRD.2010.04.0055

30. Morone, G., Masiero, S., Werner, C., Paolucci, S. Advances in neuromotor stroke rehabilitation. BioMed Research International. 2014; 2014(236043):1–2.

31. Vorobiev, A.A., Petrukhin, A.V., Zasypkina, O.A., Krivonozhkina, P.S., Pozdnyakov, A.M. Exoskeleton as a new tool in the habilitation and rehabilitation of disabled people. Modern Technologies in Medicine. 2015; 7(2):185–197.

32. Tkachenko, P.V., Daminov, V.D., Karpov, O.E. Synchronized use of an exoskeleton with functional electrical stimulation in patients with consequences of spinal cord injury. Bulletin of Rehabilitation Medicine. 2018; 3: 123–130.

33. Hidler, J.M., Hamm, L.F., Lichy, A.L., Groah, S.L. Automating activity-based interventions: The role of robotics. Journal of Rehabilitation Research and Development. 2008; 45(2):337–344. DOI: 10.1682/JRRD.2007.01.0020

34. Hesse, S., Heb, A., Werner, C., Kabbert, N., Bushfort, R. Effect on arm function and cost of robot-assisted group therapy in subacute patients with stroke and a moderately to severely affected arm: a randomized controlled trial. Clinical Rehabilitation. 2014; 28(7):637–647. DOI: 10.1177/0269215513516967

35. Mehrholz, J., Platz, T., Kugler, J., Pohl, M. Electromechanical and robot-assisted arm training for improving arm function and activities of daily living after stroke. The Cochrane Database of Systematic Reviews. 2008. CD006876. URL: https://pubmed.ncbi.nlm.nih.gov/30175845/ DOI: 10.1002/14651858.CD006876.pub5.

36. Rahaman, A., Tasnim, S., Majumdar, Md. S. H., Hossen, E., Islam (Rafiq), Md. R., "A comprehensive study on excessive mobile phone use and preventive measures", International Journal of Modern Education and Computer Science (IJMECS). 2020; 12(3):33–39.doi: 10.5815/ijmecs.2020.03.05

37. Marie, M. J., Mahdi, S. S., Tarkan, E. Y., "Intelligent control for a swarm of two wheel mobile robot with presence of external disturbance", International Journal of Modern Education and Computer Science (IJMECS). 2019; 11(11):7–12.DOI: 10.5815/ijmecs.2019.11.02

38. Khan, Md. Y. A., Sayed, Md. A., "A simple software engineering environment for coming decades", International Journal of Education and Management Engineering (IJEME), 2017; 7(1):46–53.doi:10.5815/ijeme.2017.01.05

39. Shushardzhan, S.V., Petoukhov, S.V. Engineering in the scientific music therapy and acoustic biotechnologies. In: Hu Z., Petoukhov S., He M. (eds) Advances in Artificial Systems for Medicine and Education III. AIMEE 2019. Advances in Intelligent Systems and Computing. 2020; 1126:273–282. Springer, Cham.

CHAPTER 6

Home-Automated Robot Massaging for Pandemics

Chunxu Li and Shuo Zhu

*School of Engineering, Computing and Mathematics,
University of Plymouth Plymouth, UK*

CONTENTS

In this chapter, a novel force sensing and robotic learning algorithm based teaching interface for home-automated robot massaging has been proposed. For the teaching purposes, a human operator physically holds the end-effector of the robot to perform the demonstration. At this stage, the end position data are outputted and sent to be segmented via the Finite Difference (FD) method. Dynamic movement primitive (DMP) is utilised to model and generalise the human-like movements. In order to learn from multiple demonstrations, Dynamic Time Warping (DTW) is used for the preprocessing of the data recorded on the robot platform, and Gaussian Mixture Model (GMM) is employed for the evaluation of DMP to generate multiple patterns after the completion of the teaching process. After that, Gaussian Mixture Regression (GMR) algorithm is applied to generate a synthesised trajectory to minimise position errors. Then a hybrid position/force controller is integrated to track the desired trajectory in the task space considering the safety of human–robot interaction. The validation of our proposed method has been performed and proved by conducting massage tasks on a KUKA LBR iiwa robot platform.

6.1 INTRODUCTION

With requirements to improve life quality, smart homes and healthcare have gradually become a future lifestyle. In particular, service robots with human behavioural sensing for private or personal use in the home have attracted a lot of research attention thanks to their advantages in relieving high labour costs and the fatigue of human assistance [1]. A key benefit of this approach is that the high-intensity dosing is vital for optimum outcome in rehabilitation. The problem is that achieving these high-dosage levels is extremely difficult using traditional techniques. With an aging population, and increasing numbers of people with physical disability living in the community, the demand for this increased input grows, while contextual and job-related demands remain the same. That makes the problem of meeting intensity demands – without increasing physical strain on clinicians and paid/unpaid carers – a major challenge. Hence, it is significant to build a novel integrated robotic therapy platform with rehabilitation and massaging functions in smart homes to break through the above-mentioned limits that are proving to be barriers to achieving optimal rehabilitation outcomes in people with significant disability.

Movement is a necessary way to directly produce skill effects. The motion model generates a continuous robot space state representation skill offline or online, with clear meanings related to the physical system, such as position, attitude and contact force. Generally, the motion is assumed to be nonlinear. The motion model mainly includes two categories: trajectory encoding modelling and dynamic system modelling. Trajectory encoding is a compact mathematical model that represents the shape, constraints and other information of the trajectory [2]. When the human operators teach and store one or more specific fixed trajectories to the robot, then the robot can accurately reproduce the trajectory when the motion skills are executed. Calinon et al. [3] used trajectory encoding with a multivariate Gaussian mixture model (GMM), which expresses the trajectory in a fixed coordinate system. However, considering reality, the trajectory often needs to be expressed in different reference coordinate systems, so the transformation relationship of the reference coordinate system may also change. Thus, in [4], they proposed task-parameterised Gaussian Mixture Model (TP-GMM). Wherein, the origin and rotation transformation matrix of the coordinate system are used as the task parameters in the model, which allows the observation and reproduction of the motion trajectory in different reference coordinate systems. However, the trajectory encoding modelling method only explicitly generates a fixed trajectory. When the robot is disturbed and deviates from the trajectory, the trajectory cannot be adjusted in real time, and a new trajectory needs to be regenerated.

The dynamic system is automatically evolved according to certain rules [5]. Compared with the trajectory encoding, there are two main differences: the dynamic system does not explicitly depend on the time variable, only the relationship between the spatial state and its time derivative [6]; the dynamic system can be online. It has the ability to get ground generation trajectory and online adaptive ability for disturbance. Dynamic movement primitive DMP was proposed by Ijspeert et al. [7] in 2002 as a dynamic system model that can generate trajectories of arbitrary shapes, where its basic idea is to drive a transform system with a canonical system. Nanayakkara et al. [8] proposed a Mixture of motor primitives (MoMP), using Gaiting network to calculate the weight of each DMP in the current state. Ideally, the Gaiting network should only choose one DMP implementation. However, the reality is more complicated, in order to achieve good generalised performance, MoMP weights the output of all DMPs based on the weight of the output of the gated network to obtain the final output. In [9], the coordination matrix is used to represent the coupling relationship between multiple DMPs corresponding to multiple degrees of freedom, and the iterative dimensionality reduction method is used to reduce the unnecessary degrees of freedom in the cooperation matrix, which is beneficial to enhance the learning efficiently. DMP mainly depends on the target state and weight coefficient. The former is determined by the environment or setting. The latter can learn from the teaching trajectory based on the linear weighted regression (LWR) method. However, the LWR can only learn the DMP model parameters from a single demonstration [10].

This chapter mainly presents two aspects of research, which are the theory of hybrid force/position control with direct human–robot interaction and the experimental studies on a real robotic platform.

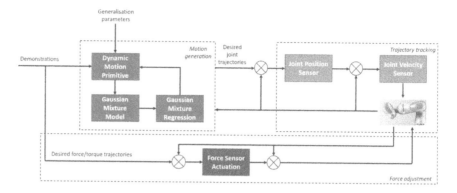

FIGURE 6.1   Diagram of the proposed control architecture.

The motion planning is performed in 3D task space, where the GMM is employed to evolute the DMP to learn from multiple demonstrations, and GMR is used for the reproduction of the generalised trajectory with a smaller error. For the force input aspects, a hybrid force/position controller is introduced to ensure the safety of direct human–robot interaction. An overview of the presented control architecture is shown in Figure 6.1. The contributions of this chapter are summarised as follows:

1. This chapter employs a teaching interface to perform the robot massaging under the demonstrations of the human operator, the experimental studies show that after teaching process, the robot can generate an even smoother trajectory that is strictly along what is requested to be followed.

2. The application of the hybrid force/position control scheme takes care of the safety issues and achieves massage services performing without knowing subject profiles.

3. The generalisation functions of our proposed method supplies a more flexible and convenient option with only once teaching for multiple tasks to the carers and patients, which promotes the user experiences.

6.2 DATA PREPROCESSING

6.2.1 Motion Skills Segmentation

FD approximates the derivative by the limitable variance and finds an estimated solution for the differential equation. The differential form, especially, is to substitute the differential with a finite difference and the derivative with a finite differential quotient, so as to roughly change the fundamental formula and limit state (usually the differential equation) into the differential equation (Algebraic equation) [11]. The solution of the differential equations problem is updated so that the algebraic equations problem is resolved.

Segmentation of skills is usually a complicated and systematic process, which requires more time and efforts on its algorithms designing. For such a complex method, it is often with difficulties in setting the priori parameters. Considering the situation that the massaging motion is planned on a horizontal plane and the force is applied into vertical direction of that plane, hence during the massaging tasks, it is easy to track for the system at which point the position being massaged has been changed. Because its position changing represents the value varying in z coordinates. Consequently, a simple segmentation method (FD) is employed in this chapter. In view of $y_i = f(z_i)$ relies upon the z_i variables, where z_i denotes the coordinate values in the vertical direction at the i_{th} time series and y_i represents the corresponding spatial sequence of the whole dataset. If z_i is changed into z_{i+1}, the corresponding changes in the whole dataset is $df(z_i) = f(z_{i+1}) - f(z_i)$ and d is the differentiation operator. Difference has a differential-like arithmetic value. This displays the following equation [12]:

$$f'(z_i) = df(z_i) = y'_i \approx \frac{y_{i+1} - y_i}{z_{i+1} - z_i} \tag{6.1}$$

where one significant massaging aspect is that the endpoint would be lifted once every single massaging task is done. The 'z' alignment values of the experimental data are thus viewed as the segmentation reference. We've received pursuing the FD:

$$\xi(y'_i) = \text{sign}\left(\left|y'_i\right| - \theta\right) \tag{6.2}$$

where ξ is the gaping variable, θ is a constant, we could modify the segmented characters, such as, θ, here $\theta = 0.5$ by giving different values of θ, sign is the Signum function and for each component of ξ the formulation could be described as following:

$$\text{sign}(\xi) = \begin{cases} -1 & \text{if } \xi < 0, \\ 0 & \text{if } \xi = 0, \\ 1 & \text{if } \xi > 0. \end{cases} \tag{6.3}$$

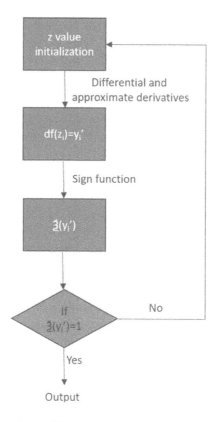

FIGURE 6.2   The flowchart of the segmentation.

Up to now, the segmented motion trajectories sign(ξ) for massaging have been outputted to different local text files for the use of GMM and DMP generalisation, which correspond to the 'z' coordinate information in the robot space, suddenly and sharply rising, which implies every time the massaging for one position was done. The flowchart of the segmentation is shown in Figure 6.2.

6.2.2 Alignment of Time Series

DTW employed in this chapter is to align the outputted trajectories curves in the form of $W = \{w_1, w_2, \cdots, w_p, \cdots, w(p)\}$ in which $w(p) = (i_p, j_p)$ denotes the match variable in [13]. In this situation, the skewed characteristic W is required to reduce the discrepancy between the pending trajectory and the reference trajectory. The formula is therefore described as:

$$D = \min \sum_{k=1}^{K} d\big[w(p)\big] \tag{6.4}$$

where $d[w(p)] = d[T_i(p), R_j(p)]$ represents the measured distance from the $i(p)^{th}$ featured point of the pending trajectory to the $j(p)^{th}$ featured point of the reference trajectory, which is normally described by a square measure specified as follows:

$$d[w(p)] = [T_i(p) - R_j(p)]^2 \qquad (6.5)$$

We need to construct a matrix grid of $m \times n$ in order to coordinate the two specimens, the matrix element (i, j) represents the range $d(T_i, R_j)$ between the two points T_i and R_j and each matrix element (i, j) represents the alignment of points R_j and R_j. DTW aims to find a direction which reflects the matched points for both samples to be determined via several grid points. First we illustrate, as $D_{Acc}(i, j)$, the total minimum range between the two trajectories, then we consider this [14]:

$$D_{Acc}(i, j) = d(T_i, R_j) + \min_{(q_i, q_j)}\left[D_{Acc}(q_i, q_j) \right] \qquad (6.6)$$

where (q_i, q_j) belongs to the set of points between $(1,1)$ and (i, j) within a certain direction. From the above components it can be seen that the average cumulative distance of the (i, j) element is linked not only to the regional distance $d(T_i, R_j)$ of the own values T_i, R_j, but also to the total cumulative distance earlier than this stage in the coordinate system.

We thus assume that $(i, j-1)$, $(i-1, j)$ and $(i-1, j-1)$ for any point $c(p) = (i, j)$ within the coordinate system may enter the preceding point of $c(p)$, so the choice of the preceding variable also needs to agree with the above three factors. We may measure the corresponding DTW range between the test pattern vector and the comparison model vector, as shown below, according to the formula below:

$$D' = D_{Acc}(L_1, L_2). \qquad (6.7)$$

6.3 TRAJECTORY GENERATION

DMP is an innovative model [15] dynamic system learned from biological research that learns from motor primitives. The definition of dynamic primitive can be separated into two groups, one of which is to use different formulas based on dynamic system to represent the state; the other is to produce the track by interpolation through the interpolation points [16]. DMP is made up of two parts: the transformed model r and the canonical framework h. The equation is shown as follows:

$$\dot{s} = h(s) \qquad (6.8)$$

$$\dot{t} = r(t, s, w) \tag{6.9}$$

where t and s are the transformed process states and the canonical function, the canonical system output variable h is referred to as w.

The canonical model is defined by an exponential differential equation, which is given by:

$$\tau\dot{s} = -\alpha_f s \tag{6.10}$$

where s is a step function varying from 0 to 1, $\tau > 0$, α_f is a temporal scaling variable and a balanced component.

The transformed model consists of two nonlinear term sections and a Cartesian space spring damping mechanism, the formulas are defined as [15]:

$$\tau\dot{v} = k(g - p) - cv + X(g - p_0) \tag{6.11}$$

$$\tau\dot{p} = v \tag{6.12}$$

where p_0 is the starting position, $p \in R$ is the Cartesian position, $v \in R$ is the end-effector velocity of the robot, g is the goal, k is the spring variable and c is the damping factor. X is a conversion method of dynamic nonlinear structures capable of transforming the outcomes of the canonical model found in the following formula:

$$X = \sum_{i=1}^{N} w_i l(s) \tag{6.13}$$

where the GMM number is N, $w_i \in R$ is the weights, and l is the uniform radial variable value that can be supplied as follows:

$$l(s) = \frac{\exp\left(xh_i \left(s - c_i\right)^2\right)}{\sum_{m=1}^{N} \exp\left(xh_m \left(s - c_m\right)^2\right)} \tag{6.14}$$

where $c_i > 0$ are the centres and $h_i > 0$ are the widths of the functions of the Gaussian foundation. N is the number of functions in Gaussian.

In addition, we can use the weight variable to produce motions by specifying the starting point of the canonical process ($s=0$) X_0 and aim g, which is the canonical system integration. The theory of DMP is to measure the nonlinear transition feature X by observing the presenter's movements. Nonetheless, there are drawbacks in developing a multi-demonstration conversion model, which is why the GMM is used to solve the above problems [17].

GMM's parameter estimation is the method by which the design parameters are obtained under certain conditions. In fact, it is the process of knowing the parameters of the model, namely the method of resolving $\lambda = \{\mu_i, \Sigma_i, \omega_i\}$ to bring the GMM sequence of observation [18]. The most commonly employed parameter estimation is the total probability approximation process. The basic idea is to consider the system parameter λ when the peak likelihood of GMM is obtained by providing the observation sequence X obtained by DMP from the previous chapter, then λ is the model. The optimum function, λ, defines to the maximum extent practicable the distribution of the observed string.

The end aim of the total probability calculation after providing the training information is to seek a template variable that maximizes the GMM's likelihood. For a training vector series of $X = \{x_1, x_2 ... x_D\}$ of duration D, it is possible to describe the likelihood of GMM as:

$$P(X \mid \lambda) = \prod_{t=1}^{D} P(X_t \mid \lambda) \qquad (6.15)$$

Then the parameter λ keeps continuously updated until a set of parameters λ is found to maximize $P(X \mid \lambda)$, which is:

$$\hat{\lambda} = \arg\max_{\lambda} P(X \mid \lambda) \qquad (6.16)$$

For the convenience of analysis, $P(X \mid \lambda)$ usually takes its log likelihood, then we have:

$$\log(P(X \mid \lambda)) = \sum_{t=1}^{D} \log P(X_t \mid \lambda) \qquad (6.17)$$

The Expectation Maximisation (EM) algorithm can be used for parameter estimation provided that there is a relatively complex nonlinear interaction between the probability function and the template parameters, and the peak value cannot be determined according to the standard probability estimation process. The EM algorithm is in essence an iterative method for calculating the probability model's maximum likelihood. The process of each iteration is to estimate the unknown data distribution based on the parameters that have been acquired, and then calculate the new model parameters under the maximum likelihood condition. Let the initial model parameter be λ, which satisfies:

$$P(X|\lambda')\ddot{O}P(X|\lambda) \tag{6.18}$$

Next we calculate the new model variable λ' according to the equation above and then use the λ' parameter as the original parameter for the next iteration. It iteratively iterates until the state of convergence is met. Here, we assume a Q function that represents the E phase of the EM process shown below:

$$Q(\lambda,\lambda') = \sum_{i=1}^{M} P(X,i|\lambda)\log P(X,i|\lambda) \tag{6.19}$$

where i is an elusive and unpredictable secret country. $Q(\lambda,\lambda')$ corresponds to all observable data's log likelihood assumptions. Calculating the maximum value of $Q(\lambda,\lambda')$ increasing give the maximum log likelihood of the observed data, which is the M stage of the EM process. It is possible to obtain replacement formulas (1.15) and (1.16) for equations (1.19):

$$Q(\lambda,\lambda') = \sum_{i=1}^{M}\sum_{t=1}^{T} r_t(i)\log\omega_i b_i(x) \tag{6.20}$$

$$r_t(i) = P(X_t,i|\lambda) \tag{6.21}$$

Then the approximate values of each variable are computed according to E and M. Phase E calculates the posterior likelihood of the t_{th} test X_t of the training data according to the Bayesian equation in the i_{th} state; phase M first uses the Q method to extract the three parameters independently and then evaluate the corresponding figures. To re-evaluate the variables, iteratively perform measures E and M. The loop is halted when the peak value of the likelihood function is reached.

The first step when using the EM method to calculate the GMM parameters is to determine the number of Gaussian components in the GMM, such as system M order and model initial parameter λ [19]. Based on the actual situation, such as the sum of training data, it is appropriate to choose the order M of the template. The most widely employed approach for the model's initial variable λ is the K-means algorithm. Currently, the K-means algorithm is the simplest and most effective classification algorithm, commonly used in different models [20]. The GMM used in this chapter chooses the basic parameters using the K-means method. The K-means algorithm partitions the information into K clusters according to the in-cluster number of squares in the category theory. After using the K-means method to cluster the feature vectors, the mean and variance of each group are determined and the percentage of each class 'feature vectors' is calculated as the blending weight [21]. The average, variance and combined weight can be then collected as the predicted values. Finally, by applying the GMR, the same theory as our previous work [22], the reconstructed motion trajectories can be then obtained.

6.4 HYBRID FORCE/POSITION CONTROL

The robot kinematics model of n DOF robot is presented in the subsequent form:

$$x(t) = \Psi(\Theta) \tag{6.22}$$

where $x(t) \in R^n$ represents the position and direction vector and $\Theta \in R^n$ represents the joint angle vector. And the inverse kinematics are:

$$\Theta(t) = \Psi^{-1}(x). \tag{6.23}$$

Thus the derivative of (1.23) can be rewritten as:

$$\dot{x}(t) = J(\Theta)\dot{\Theta} \tag{6.24}$$

where $J(\Theta)$ is the Jacobian matrix of the robot. Moreover differentiating (1.24), we can get:

$$\ddot{x}(t) = \dot{J}(\Theta)\dot{\Theta} + J(\Theta)\ddot{\Theta}. \tag{6.25}$$

The relationship between wrench and joint force can be described as:

$$T_{ext} = J^{T}(\Theta)f. \tag{6.26}$$

In addition, the robot manipulator dynamics in joint space is:

$$M_{\Theta}(\Theta)\ddot{\Theta} + C_{\Theta}(\Theta, \dot{\Theta})\dot{\Theta} + G_{\Theta}(\Theta) + T_{fric} = T + T_{ext} \tag{6.27}$$

where $\dot{\Theta}$ and $\ddot{\Theta}$ are the vectors of velocity and accelerations respectively. $Mq(\Theta) \in R^n$ is the inertia matrix; $C_\Theta(\Theta, \dot{\Theta})$ is the Coriolis and centripetal torque; $G_\Theta(\Theta)$ is the gravity; T is the robot torque; T_{fric} is the friction torque and T_{ext} is the external torque.

- *Property 1*: Matrix $M_\Theta(\Theta)$ is bounded above and below and positive definite symmetric.

- *Property 2*: Matrix $M_\Theta(\Theta)\ddot{\Theta} - 2C_\Theta(\Theta, \dot{\Theta})$ is skew symmetric matrix.

A force-position model of the relationship between the external force and position in joint space is:

$$D_g J(\Theta)(\ddot{\Theta}_r - |\ddot{\Theta}_g) \quad + (C_g J(\Theta) + M_g \dot{J}(\Theta))(\dot{\Theta}_r - \dot{\Theta}_g)$$
$$+ K_g(\phi(q_r) - \phi(q_g)) = -J^{-T} T_{ext} \tag{6.28}$$

where $q_g \in R^n$ and $q_r \in R^n$ are the desired trajectory generated from GMR algorithm and virtual desired trajectory. The M_g, C_g and K_g are gain matrix of the mass, damping and stiffness matrices designed by the controller, respectively.

- *Assumption 1*: c_1, c_2 and c_3 are positive constants, and both q_g and q_r are differentiable and bounded: $q_g, q_r \le c_1, \dot{\Theta}_g, \dot{\Theta}_r \le c_2, \ddot{\Theta}_g, \ddot{\Theta}_r \le c_3$.

- *Remark 1*: In the specific cases, force-position models such as damping-stiffness model and stiffness model are applied.

$$C_g(\dot{\Theta}_r - \dot{\Theta}_g) + K_g(q_r - q_g) = -T_{ext}$$
$$K_g(q_r - q_g) = -T_{ext} \tag{6.29}$$

In the case that the desired manipulator's motion is free and no external collisions are generated, we can get $q_r = q_g$; $T_{ext} = 0$. In the opposite, while there is an external collision, the robot will generate and follow the new trajectory, which is the adaptation to the force-position model and the external torque specified in [23] illustrates the relationship.

Regarding to the safety consideration, a moveable limit has been added to the KUKA iiwa platform in both of the Cartesian space, to make sure the manipulator can only reach the areas in front of it with a radian of 0.6 meters, in this case the robot manipulator cannot fully stretch. Meanwhile, the stiffness of its endpoint in all directions is set upon a reasonable level, hence participants can easily afford the force from the robot. Furthermore, by adjusting the threshold in **SafetyConfiguration.sconf** of the KUKA controller, the Collision Detection Framework can be activated. It is relevant to decide at what levels of the external force is, to lock down the robot protect the participants. Here, we set up this parameter at a low level, which avoids all the touching with high force.

6.5 EXPERIMENTAL STUDIES

6.5.1 Experiment Setup

A KUKA LBR iiwa robot, which has 7 DOFs of flexible joints, is implemented in our experimental studies to validate the proposed method. It is controlled utilising the KUKA Smartpad. A massage glove was attached to the end-effector of the robot. As can be seen from Figure 6.3, there is a

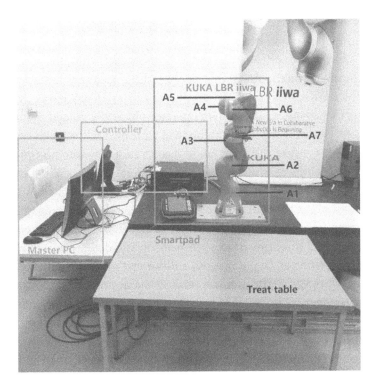

FIGURE 6.3   Illustration of the experimental system.

master computer lying by the robotic controller for data offline training purposes, which is linked to the robot controller by an Ethernet cable. The labels A1 to A7 in Figure 6.3 show the joint actuator's position with force sensor each. In addition, there is a treat table being put in front of the robot base, which is in the workspace of the robot manipulator.

The control frequency is set as 10 Hz for the KUKA LBR iiwa manipulator and the running time is limited to 30 s for the massage path tracking, and thus 300 time samplings are executed for the control loop. The endpoint stiffness in X, Y, Z directions, Roll, Pitch, Yaw orientations are setted as 1000 N/m, 1000 N/m, 100 N/m, 300 N/m, 300 N/m, 300 N/m, respectively. The control gains M_g, C_g and K_g are gain matrix of the mass, damping and stiffness and respectively set as $diag[1.0]$, $diag[1.0]$ and 0.5. The reason for setting those values are that we planned the motion path in horizontal plane using GMM – evolved DMP algorithms implementing the force in Z directions – which resulted in the impedance effectiveness in the vertical direction of the patient's back.

First of all, we conducted an experiment to test the accuracy of our proposed robotic teaching interface, where only position control was considered. As in some particular situations during the massage, the service robot may require to manipulate as accurate as our human carer, where there are specific areas of the patients required to be massaged. Thus, the accuracy of the teaching interface matters. In order to test the accuracy, firstly the position of the KUKA iiwa robot end-effector in Cartesian space was chosen as the performance index. The human operator physically guided the robot to draw a sine curve for five times in the treat table by holding its end-effector. After training process, the robot could regenerate a new smooth trajectory.

For the second experiment, one human operator physically taught the robot to do the massage movements on the first participant by holding the end-effector of the robot. After the robot being taught, a participant as well as the operator himself were massaged by the robot, wherein, the participants slowly and smoothly lifted their back up and down. Figure 6.4 shows the teaching-based massage process and we can observe that the KUKA LBR iiwa robot successfully accomplished the desired massage task with only one time teaching, consequently, our proposed massage system could automatically fit different body shapes. Meanwhile, the instantaneous external force and torque of the robot endpoint in Cartesian space were outputted to the master PC for data analysis. The real position in both of the Joint space and Cartesian space was plotted by MATLAB.

In addition, the third experiment has been conducted to validate the spatial generalisation functions of our proposed robotic teaching interface.

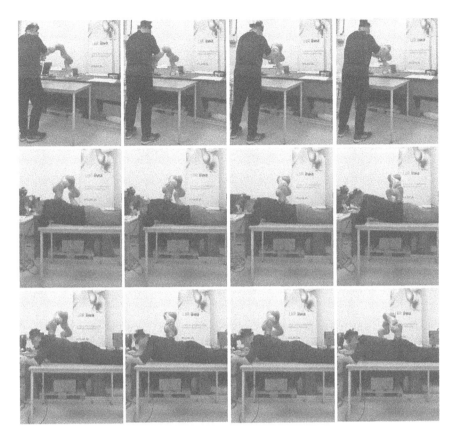

FIGURE 6.4 Experiment snapshots of the Kuka LBR iiwa manipulator for massage tasks by the proposed hybrid position/force control method.

To do this, three participants were sought to be undertaken the massage services of their shoulder by seating under the robot manipulator. The operator taught the robot to do the massage task on all the three participants with only once teaching. All the parameters kept the same as those from the second experiment. And the massage services were reproduced by the robot for all the participants one by one with different orders.

6.5.2 Experimental Results

The first group of experiments aims to verify the learning performance of our proposed teaching interface when the demonstrations are defective. To verify the learning performance of the modified DMP better, we designed a drawing task for the robot, and the experiment setup is shown in Figure 6.4. In this experiment, the robot is required to draw an image of sinusoid on the chapter after the human operator demonstrates the task five times. The parameters of the DMP model are set as: $\tau = 1$, $k = 25$, $c = 10$,

Trajectories generated by demonstrations and DMP+GMR

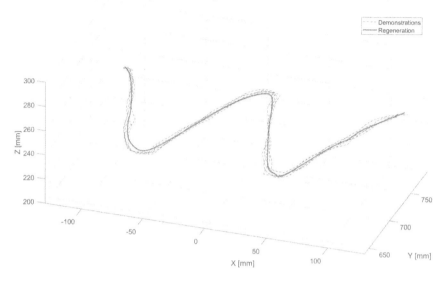

FIGURE 6.5 The trajectories of the robot endpoint in Cartesian space generated by demonstrations and the proposed teaching interface.

$\alpha_f = 8$. As is shown in Figure 6.5, the demonstrations are defective and the curves are irregular. One of the reasons is that the demonstrator is drawing on the chapter indirectly by holding the wrist of the robot, which affects the exertion of drawing skill. The demonstrations are modelled in the task space. As is shown in Figure 6.5, comparing the performance index of the demonstrations and the generated trajectory, a smooth curve is accurately retrieved from multiple demonstrations using the modified DMP without any unexpected drawing. The robot performs the drawing task after learning, and the curve that the robot draws is smoother than the demonstrations.

For the second experiment, two participants are massaged by the robot by only teaching once. During the massaging, the A7 joint of the robot is set as fixed value, because it is only related to the end-effector's orientation. Figures 6.6 and 6.7 illustrate all the 7 joints' angular data of the robot when the robot was reproducing the massage to the first and second participant, respectively. Because the massage task was first along the direction of the back of the participants and then pounded the back, thus from the Figures 6.6 and 6.7 we can see, the first joint of the robot A1 was firstly fluctuating and then kept stable; the A2, A4 and A6 joints were kept stable first and then in a fluctuating position. This is because the robot via A1 joint is moving left and right; via A2, A4 and A6 joints are moving up and down.

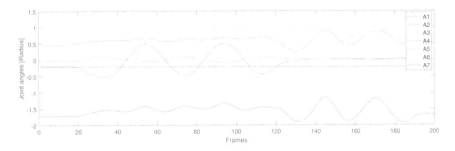

FIGURE 6.6 Angular joint values of the robot while massaging the first participant.

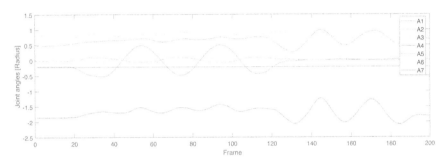

FIGURE 6.7 Angular joint values of the robot while massaging the second participant.

By comparing Figures 6.6 and 6.7, we can notice that the A2 and A4 joints were increasing, the A6 joint was decreasing during the whole massage process. It is caused by the fact that the second participant has a thicker body shape, and when the robot is in a lift-up configuration, its 6th joint will be more folded. Figures 6.8 and 6.9 show the contact force variables of the end-effector of the robot in X, Y, Z directions during the massage for the first and second participants. Here, we define that the moving direction is the positive direction of the robot endpoint. We can notice that the contact forces in X and Y directions are the positive values while in Z direction are negative values with bigger figures. This is caused during the massage paths playback process, the endpoint of the robot in Z direction met resistance comparing to its original teaching configuration. In addition, the contact force vertical to the massage paths (Z direction) also differed with two participants. Contact force variables when massaging the first participant are in the interval [−3.5 −-5] N while the variables when the robot was massaging the second participant are in [−5 −6.5] N. This is owing to the two participants have different body thickness.

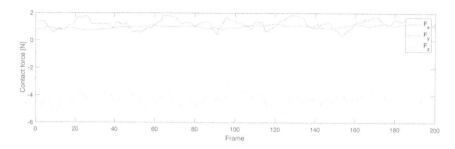

FIGURE 6.8 Contact force variables of the end-effector of the robot in X Y Z directions during the massage for the first participant.

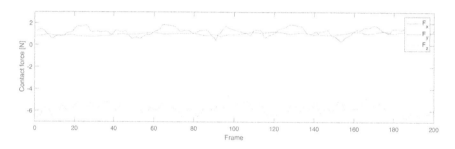

FIGURE 6.9 Contact force variables of the end-effector of the robot in X Y Z directions during the massage for the second participant.

The third test has validated the generalisation ability of our proposed massaging system. The training results are shown in Figure 6.10. The motions of the robot are regenerated from a one time teaching based demonstration, which synthesize the features of the demonstration and enable the robot to perform the massage task successfully as shown in Figure 6.10. And then the target order of the massage service is modulated to be changed.

6.5.3 Remark

Through the above conducted three experiments, it can be noticed as follows:

1. Our proposed hybrid position/force mode teaching interface was able to generate an accurate path after being taught, which reduces the errors in 3D space.

2. Our proposed hybrid position/force mode teaching interface was able to automatically and adaptively fit all body shapes with smooth force implementing.

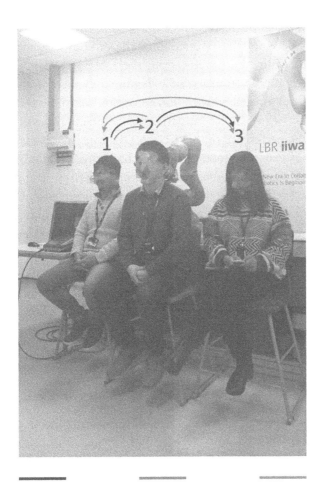

Teaching   Playback   Generalisation

FIGURE 6.10   Illustration of the third experimental process.

3. The spatial generalisation ability was validated, where the whole massage tasks can be segmented into several unit movement primitives, which can be regrouped into different orders with only one time teaching, it promoted the working flexibility.

6.6 CONCLUSION

In this chapter, an enhanced force sensing and robotic learning algorithm based robotic teaching interface has been developed to perform the massaging tasks. In the motion generation part, the discrete DMP is selected as the basic motion model, which can achieve the generalisation of the motions.

To improve the learning performance of the DMP model, the GMM and GMR are employed for the estimation of the unknown function of the motion model. With this modification, the DMP model is enabled to retrieve a better motion from multiple demonstrations of a specific task. For the force input aspects, a hybrid force/position controller is introduced to ensure the safety of direct human–robot interaction. Several experiments have been performed on the KUKA LBR iiwa robot to test the performance of our proposed methods, which has proved that our proposed method can be used to establish a novel robot learning framework for massaging and facilitate the robot learning at a higher level. Our future work will focus on combining with visual monitoring technology, where the acupuncture point and bones of the patient's back will be clearly recognised and tracked, which results in a better demonstrations for the robot to learn from.

BIBLIOGRAPHY

1. Hang Su, Andrea Mariani, Salih Ertug Ovur, Arianna Menciassi, Giancarlo Ferrigno, and Elena De Momi. Toward teaching by demonstration for robot-assisted minimally invasive surgery. *IEEE Transactions on Automation Science and Engineering*, pages 1–11. 2021.
2. Junshen Chen, Marc Glover, Chunxu Li, and Chenguang Yang. Development of a user experience enhanced teleoperation approach. In *2016 International Conference on Advanced Robotics and Mechatronics (ICARM)*, pages 171–177. IEEE, 2016.
3. Sylvain Calinon and Aude Billard. Incremental learning of gestures by imitation in a humanoid robot. In *Proceedings of the ACM/IEEE International Conference on Human-robot Interaction*, pages 255–262. ACM, 2007.
4. Joao Silvério, Leonel Rozo, Sylvain Calinon, and Darwin G Caldwell. Learning bimanual end-effector poses from demonstrations using task-parameterized dynamical systems. In *2015 IEEE/RSJ International Conference on Intelligent Robots and Systems (IROS)*, pages 464–470. IEEE, 2015.
5. Asma Ayari and Sadok Bouamama. ACD³ GPSO: automatic clustering-based algorithm for multi-robot task allocation using dynamic distributed double-guided particle swarm optimization. *Assembly Automation*, pages 235–247. 2019.
6. Chengguo Zong, Zhijian Ji, and Haisheng Yu. Dynamic stability analysis of a tracked mobile robot based on human–robot interaction. *Assembly Automation*, pages 143–154. 2019.
7. Stefan Schaal. Movement planning and imitation by shaping nonlinear attractors. In *Proceedings of the 12th Yale Workshop on Adaptive and Learning Systems*. Citeseer, 2003.

8. Thrishanta Nanayakkara, Keigo Watanabe, Kazuo Kiguchi, and Kiyotaka Izumi. *Evolving obstacle avoidance skill of a seven-link manipulator subject to constraints using an evolutionary algorithm.* pages 167–178. 2013.

9. Takamitsu Matsubara, Sang-Ho Hyon, and Jun Morimoto. Learning parametric dynamic movement primitives from multiple demonstrations. *Neural Networks*, 24(5):493–500, 2011.

10. Feifei Bian, Danmei Ren, Ruifeng Li, Peidong Liang, Ke Wang, and Lijun Zhao. An extended dmp framework for robot learning and improving variable stiffness manipulation. *Assembly Automation*, pages 85–94. 2019.

11. James R Chelikowsky, Norm J Troullier, and Yousef Saad. Finite-difference-pseudopotential method: Electronic structure calculations without a basis. *Physical Review Letters*, 72(8):1240, 1994.

12. Chunxu Li, Chenguang Yang, and Cinzia Giannetti. Segmentation and generalisation for writing skills transfer from humans to robots. *Cognitive Computation and Systems*, 1(1):20–25, 2019.

13. François Petitjean, Germain Forestier, Geoffrey I Webb, Ann E Nicholson, Yanping Chen, and Eamonn Keogh. Dynamic time warping averaging of time series allows faster and more accurate classification. In *2014 IEEE International Conference on Data Mining*, pages 470–479. IEEE, 2014.

14. Pavel Senin. Dynamic time warping algorithm review. *Information and Computer Science Department University of Hawaii at Manoa Honolulu, USA*, 855(1–23):40, 2008.

15. Stefan Schaal. Dynamic movement primitives-a framework for motor control in humans and humanoid robotics. In *Adaptive Motion ofAnimals and Machines*, pages 261–280. Springer, 2006.

16. Chunxu Li, Chenguang Yang, Jian Wan, Andy Annamalai, and Angelo Cangelosi. Neural learning and Kalman filtering enhanced teaching by demonstration for a Baxter robot. In *2017 23rd International Conference on Automation and Computing (ICAC)*, pages 1–6. IEEE, 2017.

17. Hang Su, Wen Qi, Chenguang Yang, Juan Sandoval, Giancarlo Ferrigno, and Elena De Momi. Deep neural network approach in robot tool dynamics identification for bilateral teleoperation. *IEEE Robotics and Automation Letters*, 5(2):2943–2949, 2020.

18. Kin-Fai Tong and Jingjing Huang. New proximity coupled feeding method for reconfigurable circularly polarized microstrip ring antennas. *IEEE Transactions on Antennas and Propagation*, 56(7):1860–1866, 2008.

19. Phil G Howlett, Peter J Pudney, and Xuan Vu. Local energy minimization in optimal train control. *Automatica*, 45(11):2692–2698, 2009.

20. KA Abdul Nazeer and MP Sebastian. Improving the accuracy and efficiency of the k-means clustering algorithm. In *Proceedings of the World Congress on Engineering*, volume 1, pages 1–3. Association of Engineers London, 2009.

21. Suman Tatiraju and Avi Mehta. Image segmentation using k-means cluster-ing, EM and normalized cuts. *Department of EECS*, 1:1–7, 2008.

22. Chunxu Li, Chenguang Yang, Zhaojie Ju, and Andy SK Annamalai. An enhanced teaching interface for a robot using DMP and GMR. *International Journal of Intelligent Robotics and Applications*, 2(1):110–121, 2018.

23. Michael Bernhardt, Martin Frey, Gery Colombo, and Robert Riener. Hybrid force-position control yields cooperative behaviour of the rehabilitation robot Lokomat. In *9th International Conference on Rehabilitation Robotics, 2005. ICORR 2005*, pages 536–539. IEEE, 2005.

Index

Note: Locators in *italics* represent figures and **bold** indicate tables in the text.

Milton Keynes UK
Ingram Content Group UK Ltd.
UKHW031133141024
449569UK00006B/211